KU-012-164

BRAND PACKAGING

BRAND PACKAGING

the permanent medium

HAVERING COLLEGE
OF FURTHER & HIGHER EDUCATION

LEARNING RESOURCES
CENTRE

by
Julien Behaeghel

ARCHITECTURE DESIGN AND TECHNOLOGY PRESS

H.L.

658.564

111302

First published in 1991 by
Architecture Design and
Technology Press
128 Long Acre, London WC2E 9AN

© 1991 Julien Behaeghel

ISBN 1 85454 055 6

All rights reserved; no part of this publication may be reproduced, stored in a retrieval system, or transmitted in any form or by any means, electronic, mechanical, photocopying, recording, or otherwise, without the prior written permission of the Publisher

British Library Cataloguing in Publication Data: a CIP record for this book is available from the British Library

Linotronic: Alphabet Set, London
Printed and bound in Hong Kong

CONTENTS

INTRODUCTION

Packaging is a part of our everyday life which reflects the main socio-economic trends of our time. Current popular preoccupations with ecology and phenomena endemic to pollution are represented in packaging by a return to origins illustrated by the use of 'traditional' materials and the marketing of 'old-fashioned products' evoking a nostalgia for the past.

Today, packaging is used by many consumers to assert their social status. For example, a certain brand of whiskey or a brand of cigarettes is for them an outward sign of their social rank. Similarly, people readily flaunt the names of the stores they patronize, or the brand of beer that they drink or make of car that they drive.

The many unisex products that have been launched illustrate the power of feminism and the social acceptance of homosexuality. At the same time, many products previously thought of as typically masculine or feminine are now bought by both sexes.

However, the economic role of packaging is far more important than its social role – not only is packaging necessary for the protection of goods in transport and handling, but it is also an essential element in the distribution of these goods.

It is difficult to imagine the supermarket system without packaging that is constantly being adapted to changing needs, whatever the product. A well-designed package means the correct choice of materials, a shape suitable for the demands of transport, storage and handling, as well as aesthetics which enable it to play the role of the 'silent salesman' required of packaging today.

If the preceding view, originally postulated in 1977 as an introduction to a booklet entitled 'The World of Packaging'[1], remains broadly true, one can perceive that packaging has been constantly evolving as far as materials, technology and the evolution of packaging machinery are concerned.

The package is the first and the last link in the production–distribution chain. Today it is a means of communication that, even across frontiers, acts as a vehicle for the brand personality, transcending differences of language, culture and attitude. It is the focus for the message. A functional object, following the theories of the *Bauhaus*, it has become a means of communication. A perfect medium, it is present in the stores and in our homes. We live with it constantly without once doubting that, as the focus for the message, it is the most effective form of publicity on a *per capita* basis. Pilditch writes that 'advertising messages do not have the same lasting effect as a package which is exposed to the eyes of the customer on the shelves and in shop windows for many years, it follows that the expense of designing an attractive sales promoting package is very modest per unit'.[2]

The package is a marketing and communications tool, a permanent omnipresent medium that acts as a salesman. A package designer uses this tool to express the nuances that the brand owner requires the package to communicate.

Packaging, being an excellent form of commercial medium, finds its expression in the words of McLuhan who says: 'We can no longer build serially, block by block, step by step, because instant communication ensures that all factors of the environment and of experience co-exist in a state of active interplay...'[3].

This book does not set out to analyse the technical side of packaging; this would involve too many different industrial disciplines, and there are regular international trade fairs devoted to this aspect of the business. The aim of this work is to show how packaging works as a tool of commercial communication in the light of my 30 years as a package designer, and as leader of a marvellous team of creative people to whom this book is dedicated.

I would like to thank all those colleagues who throughout the years have helped me to participate actively in the birth of a fascinating profession. My greatest thanks go to the team of Design Board/Behaeghel & Partners (DBB&P) as well as to all the clients that I have had the pleasure to work with and who have played a very special role in this interesting professional adventure.

JULIEN BEHAEGHEL

ACKNOWLEDGEMENTS

I would like to offer my sincerest thanks to all the people who helped me in the preparation of this book, especially:

Erik Vantal – cover design

Lieve Baeten – Layout

Veerle Van Malleghem – typing and text editing

Paul Battersby – translation

Dick Colian – cover and most of the photographs

and all the designers and manufacturers whose products are featured in this book.

It can be said without exaggeration that there is no such thing as a product without a package, and it is equally true that it is not possible to communicate the product effectively without linking the three different strategic areas involved. The spokes of the wheel (production, communication and market) which come together at its hub (the ultimate product) must communicate the same message by different means. The manufacturer defines his business strategy and the media communicate the product in a way that meets the market demand.

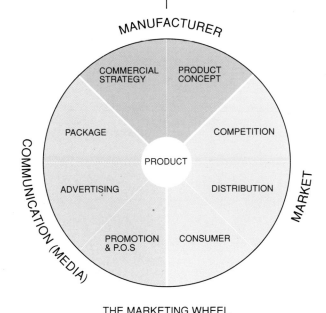

THE MARKETING WHEEL

1.1
THE MANUFACTURER

Product quality is an essential element in any business strategy. Slavish copies of existing products, without any special advantages or any specific personality, cannot form the basis for any strategy worthy of the name. 'Imitation', wrote Jean-Marie Dru in his book *Le Saut Créatif*, 'is a form of business suicide. Only new ideas can arouse public interest and enable the manufacturer to seize his chance to increase market share'.[4]

As J.N. Kapferer and J.C. Thoenig say in their book *La Marque*, 'the real added value of a brand is in the product and its constant updating to improve quality, performance, usage to keep pace with changing consumer tastes and needs'[5], the manufacturer being seen by the consumer as the guarantor of the product. The product definition enables the manufacturer and consumer to identify the essential function of a product, its unique selling proposition (USP), the end result the consumer wants. This definition positions the product in its market sector at a price level compatible with the market situation (everyday consumer product, luxury item or down market product).

1.1.1
Brand strategy or company strategy?
As well as supporting the brand and the company identity, the package fits naturally into the general policy of presenting the corporate face of any industrial company. A corporate image is presented via various

different means of communication which must be coherent and homogeneous to be efficient, that is to say, the brand or company identity must be communicated following a predetermined visual discipline. The elements of a brand or company identity generally consist of symbols, a brand or company logo, colour codes – a collection of symbols and colours that identify one brand or manufacturer from all the other brands or manufacturers in one or more markets. Whether it is a brand strategy or a company strategy, it is generally defined in function by the type of product or by the area of activity of a manufacturer. A large distribution chain or industrial company often employs a policy of company identity (e.g. IBM, Kodak, Delhaize), whereas a producer of everyday consumer goods (e.g. Procter & Gamble or Unilever) adopts a strategy of using brand identity.

Whichever strategy is used by the manufacturer, it must be defined at the outset and be taken into consideration when a package is being designed. In the case of a brand strategy, the brand identity should appear in the same way on every product in the range, and if possible in all markets where the product is sold. In the case of a company strategy any products made by that manufacturer should convey the company identity.

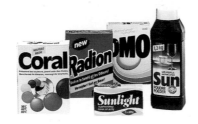

1.2
MEDIA

Total communication is fashionable at the moment, and is in fact well named. It is a judicious harmonization of all the different levels of communication that affect a single product. However, each area of communication has its own methods which should not be confused.

1.2.1
The package: an ongoing and repetitive medium

The silent medium of the pack works through repetition. It is continually seen on shop shelves and appears in advertising as a visual reminder of the product. It is the most effective link between the manufacturer and the consumer. However, it should not be overestimated – the package can only give what it has. It is neither an advertisement nor a recipe. Too often we try to make it do too much, and frequently it is quite small. The eye can only assimilate a given amount of information in a given period and to play its role of silent salesman the pack must attract, inform and convince a potential buyer in a few seconds. It is therefore necessary to structure the visual elements in a hierarchy of importance and to eliminate any elements that may interfere with the communication of the brand

personality. The brand and its historic associations, the product definition and its USP (unique selling proposition) are the most important elements in the whole package, and they must not be sacrificed for advertising or promotional reasons. The list of essential criteria in a packaging design study is too complex to accept any considerations outside the main purpose that may damage the clarity of the message. The packaging strategy explains the personality of the product in function of the realities of the market place and excludes all general or ephemeral objectives. A package design must be long-lasting and any elements that are trivial or tied to fashion should be avoided.

1.2.2
Advertising: medium of the imagination

Like packaging, advertising must convince and motivate a potential buyer. Through words and images it must, explains Jean-Marie Dru, 'lift the brand out of the ordinary, and give it added content ... so that the subject evolves from being a product to being a brand. It is that that explains the move from the explicit to the implicit, and from the rational to the imaginary'.[6]

Thus the advertising agency defines the strategy which becomes the vehicle for the selling idea. This should not be confused with the idea that must be expressed by the package. An advertising idea can convey *joie de vivre*, softness, youth, speed, serenity etc. The package must illustrate the commodity, the essential characteristics of the product and the brand identity (not brand image, which falls more in the domain of advertising).

Communication in packaging consists of images and symbols; the need for conciseness excludes complex visuals and complicated explanations. If the advertising strategy is relatively permanent, the way in which it is executed can often vary with time; this is not the case with a packaging strategy which must convey the idea of the product for what is usually a long period, even if successive visual changes may be necessary.

1.2.3
Sales promotion: medium of the moment

Sales promotion consists of periodically increasing the sales of a product by using techniques such as price reductions, demonstrations, special offers, etc. It has the objective of motivating sales and distribution networks. A pack may incorporate certain elements of the sales promotion strategy, such as special price offers, or promotional patches. The package or one of its constituent

elements may also generate the theme of the promotion: a reusable carton or a package that serves as a tool or as a dosing device are possible examples. The package is the least costly means of sales promotion, but a package can be destroyed by promotions or by the random and temporary introduction of graphic elements that may detract from the overall brand image of the product. What can be said about manufacturers who are forced to adopt a policy of permanent promotions for the sake of maintaining a profitable sales level? Promotions that consist of permanent price offers or sporadic free gifts can only damage the brand image and destroy the manufacturer's credibility.

1.2.4
Point of Sale (POS): medium of visibility

The objective of POS is to draw attention to the product within the sales area by separating it from competition (end-of-aisle or free-standing), or by using a display (counter or floor) which lifts the product out of the competitive environment. The package and its display form a unit that helps to reinforce the brand identity, and should be conceived with as much care and attention to quality as the pack itself. For reasons of internal politics, displays have virtually disappeared from the

large supermarkets and today their use is often limited to small specialized shops.

'At the moment that you buy it "with your eyes", the sales decision depends on the visual power of the package'.[7] A good product display in the sales area can only help, especially where impulse buying is concerned. This constitutes a significant percentage of sales for many products, but whatever POS material is used, the package remains the fundamental sales tool.

1.3
THE MARKET

The market is the third dimension of the marketing wheel and is, in effect, the only one that the manufacturer cannot influence. Although the competition, the distributors and the consumers are outside of his control, they still represent essential factors in the sales strategy. The manufacturers should pay constant attention to the views of these invaluable people.

1.3.1
Distribution
The modern distribution system gives nothing for free. It imposes its own rules on producers, and any product that does not perform well in terms of sales volume is quickly done away with; for example a pro-duct which does not have a broad enough consumer base. Distributors are well-equipped to measure market reaction, and the Nielsen ratings, and more recently, bar code scanner returns are two of the marketing man's basic tools. The real proof of the value of a product is the test market. A good distribution network and good relations with distributors are vital for the success of any business plan. An excellent package can do nothing if it is not on the shelf. It is however true that 'the distributor communicates primarily via in-store advertising and only secondarily via the products',[8] often using brand-name products to promote sales of his own brand by slavishly imitating them ... another way of recognizing the power of the big brands. A package cannot be evaluated on a conference room table; the real environment of consumer products is the supermarket or department store. Only in these surroundings can one properly evaluate the effectiveness of the brand personality and the brand identity of a package, presupposing that display conditions are taken into account at the creative stage. It is always useful not only to do regular store-checks, but also to ask distributors and store managers how a package fulfils their requirements; sometimes these replies can throw a completely new light on a package design development.

1.3.2
The competition

The competition constitutes the physical environment, the background in which the pack must live and evolve and is the context that often determines important changes to a package. A pack is not created to stay the same; to remain effective it must develop to keep pace with changes made by the competition, especially if they adopt a similar strategy to your own brand, or if they try to create confusion in the mind of the consumer by imitating the main characterisitcs of your package. Above all, the package must be visible, it must stand out from the mass of competition – in short, it must be different.

A question often asked is, when to change a package? The answer is simple: when your pack can be confused with its main competitors, or when sales start to decline; in fact, when the package no longer supports the brand strategy or reflects its ideal personality. A change to the product, a change to the structure or material of the package, and any development of sales systems or changes to consumer habits are imperative reasons to modify the pack to incorporate these new characteristics. A package is constantly evolving because it lives in an environment of perpetual mutation.

1.3.3
The consumer

The consumer is the person to whom the message being transmitted by the manufacturer via the package is destined. Thus it is essential to understand the consumer both on a social and cultural level and from a product usage standpoint. It is important to respect the consumer and to remain constantly aware of his or her criticisms and aspirations, while avoiding a package that deceives. Environmental preoccupations must be taken into account; the product, its content, and usage information should be clearly presented.

Knowledge of the consumer enables the manufacturer to define the market sector, the socio-economic profile of the buyer and the main sales message to use.

The consumer is not identical from one geographic area to another, and the fragmentation of the buying public in most markets is paralysing the traditional media. This reinforces the convergent role of the package, which is becoming increasingly the lowest common denominator of product communication on an international level. In other words, the more the consumer base diversifies, the more the package becomes the main vehicle for the brand image.

In conclusion, the marketing wheel only works if all of its components are balanced. If it is true that a product cannot exist without a package, it can only become known if advertising makes the market aware of its existence. It can only be present at the POS if the distribution chain is well-organized and efficiently run by a well-motivated sales force; it can only play its role of silent salesman if sales promotion gives prominence to the product in the eyes of distributors and consumers. Finally, the product will only be purchased if the price is in correct relationship with the promised quality level and that of the competition.

This chapter deals with the physical and commercial functions of the package and the ways in which they affect the manufacturer, distributor and consumer.

Communication is the function that is most underused or badly used in packaging. This does not exclude other functions, it merely implies that they should be treated with care and creativity.

An interesting book, *Le Pack*,[9] subdivides the functions of a package into technical (i.e. conservation and distribution) and marketing (i.e. impact, market sector, information, positioning and use). They can be thought of as physical functions as opposed to commercial ones: manufacture, protection, transport, storage and content versus ease of use, aesthetics, information, price and ecology.

2.1
THE PHYSICAL FUNCTIONS

2.1.1
Manufacturing/ economics

The manufacture of a package is influenced by a number of factors: the product (which affects the choice of materials), the manufacturing processes used by the producer, and the level of technology available to the packaging manufacturer.

Whatever the product, the designer can resolve these problems in a creative way by harmonizing the structural, material and technical aspects of a package. Technology used properly creates packaging that is more functional and more economic to produce. Lightweight glass is an excellent example, where combining a carefully designed shape that allows better distribution of glass in the mould with improved technology results in the saving of many tons of glass a year.

In bottle manufacture, a round form is more economic than a square, oval or a polygonal one, but it can still have a profile which has character, such as the Loburg beer bottle (Belgian premium beer produced by Interbrew) which is distinctive among its hundreds of competitors.

For plastic containers, a symmetrical form is more economical to produce than an asymmetric one, and it is worth remembering that the container closure often represents a significant part of the total cost (section 2.2.4).

In carton and label manufacture intelligent design of the cutting form and carefully thought-out grouping can save paper and board, just as a carton manufactured in one piece is more economic to make than one assembled from a number of elements. There are many other way to economize at all levels of carton manufacture, such as multilingual packages, rationalization of printing methods, reduction in the number of colours used, centralization and co-ordination of all production phases (i.e. manufacture, photoengraving and printing as well as the centralization of design). Although the economic function is important, one should beware of false economies: one or two extra colours could help create a more convincing carton that better conveys the quality and originality of the product.

2.1.2
Protection/ preservation

In its long journey from the manufacturer to the consumer a package is handled many times and is submitted to the vicissitudes of transport and storage, making the choice of materials, closure or sealing and type of palletization important elements in ensuring its protection. This is more complex than it appears, as the choice of material must serve the function of the nature of the product, but is often influenced by its 'qualitative' value. Glass, although a stable material, is more fragile than plastics or composites, and is still preferred for packaging perfumes or traditional drinks such as beer, wine and liqueurs. The role of closures is ambivalent: the easy opening required of preserve jars, aluminium

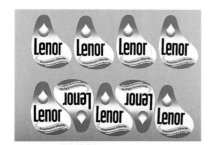

cans or beer bottles is completely contrary to the high security or tamper-proof closures used for dangerous products, pharmaceuticals, and processed foods.

A package can act as a barrier to oils and greases, acids, gases and water vapour; it can resist tearing, shock, high or low temperatures, or it can be perfectly hermetic, rigid, light or shiny; all of these qualities are major attributes for any effectively designed package.

2.1.3
Transport/storage

The demands of transport and storage have lead to the development of numerous bulk-packaging and palletization systems, which fulfil their primary role of protecting the product during handling and transport also play an important role in reinforcing the product identity. For certain types of product the pallet or the shipping carton can become a display unit at the point of sale, and although the materials and printing methods diminish the graphic quality of these shipping cartons, their design is still important; whether a box, a multipack, a shrink-wrapped tray, a cigarette carton or beer crate, all help to reinforce the brand image and should retain the same graphics as the main pack. Indeed, the name on the shipper is often the only thing that you can see.

2.1.4
Content/format

Four basic criteria can determine the content level of a package: (i) consumer habits; (ii) regulations; (iii) price; and (iv) the commodity itself. The respective importance of these criteria varies from sector to sector and country to country, but by and large price, ease of use and storage are the most influential factors. A Tetra Brik pack for milk or fruit juice is easier to use and store than a traditional glass bottle, with the ease of shelf filling being an important factor both at distribution and consumer levels. A family or bulk-size container will always be more economic than a smaller size, but the way a product is consumed can also determine the content, as in the case of single-portion meals versus the needs of mass catering.

The outer volume of a package can be influenced by its colour or shape, and to give an impression of the same size as your competitors is justifiable as long as the package does not deceive the consumer.

2.2
THE COMMERCIAL FUNCTIONS

2.2.1
Ease of use

The handle on a 5 kg detergent carton or a beer multipack; an easy-opening preserve jar, carton or yoghurt pot; a beverage carton pouring spout or washing-up liquid dosing cap; a shoe polish tub with applicator; a square section easy to store mineral water or fruit juice bottle ... all are examples of ease of use – a top-priority function when most packages are designed. To achieve this it is necessary to analyse how the product is used, and query the function of the package. A functional package can become an inseparable part of the product as in the case of aerosols or coffee packaged in filter form.

Function can be separated into six areas: (i) materials (e.g. when a card–aluminium–plastic laminate replaces glass or metal, as for milk, fruit juices etc.); (ii) form or structure (aerosols, rigid cigarette packs, packages shaped to the hand); (iii) dispensing (pouring spouts, dosing caps, or dose-size units); (iv) open

ing/closing (easy-grip caps, ring-pull cans, crown caps, flip-top cartons); (v) a tool (shoe polish applicator, dispensing packs as for paper handkerchieves, pills, sauces etc); and (vi) secondary usage (packages that become a utensil or toy). Studying packaging from this point of view is one of the most promising ways of creating more efficient and innovative packs.

2.2.2
Aesthetics

Aesthetics underpin all commercial communication and it could be said that a package is a commercial work of art in the same way as a poster or a car body, needing very specialized know-how to meet numerous technical and legal demands. Art for art's sake is not relevant as packaging is a collection of limitations imposed by machines, printing techniques, photo-engraving, format, the distribution system etc; a designer must stay within the limits of the means at his disposal: shape, colour, texture, illustration, photography, and use them to communicate visually the product personality.

Aesthetics, through the applied arts and the discipline of the designer, are the ingredients necessary to create quality packaging. The art of our era is the art of communication and there is no reason to deny it the right to express beauty and poetry. Packaging should become an artefact as in previous times. Jocelyn de Noblet said in his pamphlet in 1989, 'we live in a type of society where the importance of material culture is ever increasing. It is becoming a matter of growing urgency to create effective brand images that re-establish the relationship between the economy and our culture.'[10] The package, with its cultural, symbolic and economic components, is one means of achieving this end.

Gift packaging deserves a special mention, as aesthetics are very important in that the 'gift' aspect provides added value to the 'product' and this should be clearly perceived by the person receiving the gift. It is sufficient to look around airport boutiques to understand the importance of gift packaging, which tends to be used permanently for such things as perfumes, expensive watches and luxury products in general, and periodically for items such as biscuits, chocolates or cigarettes. In Japan, presents traditionally given at the solstice holidays are mostly gift-packed.

2.2.3
Information

As well as the brand personality, a package must convey all the characteristics of the product as well as information about its use and method of usage, not forgetting legal and technical elements, often translations into other languages. Two errors are often made: too much information, and lack of structure in the information, whereas simplicity is often synonymous with quality, and in packaging it guarantees quick recognition when a complicated pack will not even be noticed.

A simple visual approach devoid of irrelevant information attracts the pack to consumers surrounded by thousands of other packs all vying for attention. Opt for concise

information presented in a structured way that makes essential information stand out – brand, type of product, its main characteristics, weight and sell-by date – as opposed to secondary information such as usage, contents and legal text and whenever possible replace text by an ideogram or symbol.

In the case of multilingual packaging, often used in Europe, it is not always easy to organize linguistic information. There are three general solutions: (i) a unilingual package with text in one colour that is changed for each country; (ii) a multilingual package grouping the languages of a geographic area (Northern Europe, Central Europe); or (iii) a bilingual or trilingual package (Belgium, Switzerland, Canada) dividing the languages on the two main faces of the carton.

2.2.4
Price

If it can be said that a package is the main vehicle for the brand identity, then it can also be said to be priceless. A good package promotes better distribution and wins extra sales; therefore the investment made is modest in relation to possible sales increases and the impression of added value it creates.

However, pricing is a variable function dictated by the materials chosen, the quantities produced and the manufacturing methods. Form

and format play a strong role in the price equation and for this reason it is important to establish a comparative scale of cost for the components of a package, representing from 5 to 50 per cent of the value of the product as a function of its real cost, and an average of 16 per cent in the food sector. A perfume bottle will represent a much higher percentage compared with a detergent carton and the product category can help define the factors to be considered. In the example that we show, it is interesting to note the price–content relationship and the relatively high cost of the closure compared with the other elements of the plastic bottle. The design of a package is also an excellent criterion, as a 'well-thought-out package' costs less than a 'badly or not-thought-out' carton.

2.2.5
Ecology

Bio-degradable packages, recycled products and the abandonment of certain materials or ingredients (freon gas for aerosols, phosphates for detergents etc), are some of the signs of the increasing role of ecology in packaging, which currently represents more than one third of household waste or more than 50 per cent if measured by volume. 'The protection of our environment and the fight against pollution caused by packaging is, without any doubt, a new mission assigned to the packaging world. It is our responsibility to face up to this with determination and to find solutions ...'.[11]

Recycling, Reclamation, Reduction and Recovery are known as the four R's or the four methods to reduce the solid waste impact of packaging and this will be linked with weight reductions in certain packaging and the design of refill packs to be used in conjunction with re-usable packages.

These solutions are valid in that they offer the potential to reabsorb or at least reduce waste created by the packaging industry, bearing in mind that packaging pollution represents only a small percentage (around one per cent) of environmental pollution, although it is of course rather apparent.

Packaging suppliers', packaging users' and designers' professional

CAP

HANDLE

COLOR

STRENGTH & GLOSS

SIZE IMPRESSION

0,25L   1L

associations are creating awareness of the problems among their members and working together to find the best possible solutions.

On the other hand some distribution chains have introduced 'green ranges' which give prominence to environmentally friendly products and packages, although the concept of what is a truly 'environmentally friendly' package is not necessarily easy to fully comprehend.

Packaging Week, in a special report dated February 1990, contained an especially well-thought-out and informative analysis. To sum up this subject, a quote from Leo Katan's editorial in this issue (p.1), 'Artificial recycling systems, darlings of the environmentalists usually consume fossil fuels. To assess the efficiency and justification of such a system, one must balance the recovery of material resources against use of energy'.

It is obvious that the physical and commercial functions are complementary and must be combined harmoniously in order to produce an optimum package. How to integrate these functions in order to transform the package into a 'communication tool' will be examined later.

The 'briefing' or design request is essentially the response to a series of questions which clarify and put into perspective what the package has to communicate. Who is the potential purchaser? What is the product? What is the competition? What are the product's characteristics? What is the communication strategy? What are the physical, technical and legal limitations? In short, what does the package have to communicate to the consumer? For example, it can be to communicate the main benefit of the product or its principal usage area, or attributes associated with the product such as the aroma of coffee or the thirst-quenching freshness of a cool drink. Objectives such as 'should have quality, shelf impact, differentiation from competition' are common objectives to any packaging brief and are not specific enough.

Great care and thought should be given to the briefing, as it forms the basis of the dialogue between the manufacturer and designer enabling the manufacturer to identify the problem and the designer to determine the best visual way of communicating the brand personality. The objective is not to manipulate the consumer, but rather to make him or her aware that a particular product has an 'individuality' and is 'different' from its competition even if as Vance Packard observes in *La Persuasion Clandestine*, we are all

'lovers of image inclined to act impulsively'[12], nothing prevents us from communicating the product concept honestly and persuasively.

The design request used by Design Board/Behaeghel & Partners covers the following four sections, and is constantly updated to keep pace with changing needs: (i) general marketing criteria; (ii) brand and packaging strategy; (iii) creative information; and (iv) technical information.

3.1 'MR AND MRS EVERYBODY'

For the majority of consumer products the 'target consumer' is 'Mr and Mrs Everybody', a demographic composite of a country or of several countries and indistinct in that they cover all socio-economic groups and often combine different nationalities. Even if it is possible to identify certain narrow target groups, such as the unmarried, children in different age groups, doctors etc, the majority of packages must communicate to a widely varied audience, although *World Packaging News* for September, 1989, says that the most you can do to define this is to divide European consumers on a north/south basis in terms of lifestyle and mentality.[13]

In addition, it is important to identify the target consumer, to understand the marketing criteria such as positioning of the brand, its image, content and reputation, its strengths and weaknesses versus competition, how it is distributed and priced, as well as being aware of the main market trends. The analysis of Chaudfontaine mineral water is an example from the Belgian market. When evaluated, brand awareness was weak (51 per cent). It was second in sales to Spa and its main competitors were the French mineral waters (Evian, Vittel). The brand image had little content, being an aging image mainly associated with carbonated soft drinks rather than table water, with a distribution system based on door-to-door deliveries and small corner shops and only a 7 per cent presence in super and hypermarkets. Its pricing level is the same or cheaper than the competition, in a market growing at 2 per cent per annum. With a consumer base of young adults and children, its main advantage is that it is a natural spring water, although this does not give it an advantage against the competition.

This information enabled the manufacturer and designer to situate the product in its sales environment, as J.-M. Dru remarked, 'The positioning of a product is simply its place versus competition in the mind of the consumer. To position a product is to make a choice. This choice is the source of differentiation'.[14]

The package designer should define the packaging strategy as a function of the essential product characteristic or product benefit, its quality level and the different levels of communication necessary: family, variety and sub-varieties – the brand strategy is the heart of the message. In the case of Chaudfontaine it was to express the purety and lightness of spring water using the brand symbol (a dove) while respecting a consumer code unique to Belgium of blue for normal water and red for carbonated water. The brand strategy is supported by the general marketing strategy which defines market penetration, sales targets and profit levels; the advertising strategy and media plan results in a 'selling idea' to make consumers aware of the product, in the case of Chaudfontaine using the idea of 'water for life', associating the purity of the product with all different age groups (J. Binon, the Belgian advertising agency for Chaudfontaine).

However, none of these strategies can succeed without an excellent national/international distribution system, an important matter for Chaudfontaine because of the continuing reduction in door-to-door deliveries. The promotion

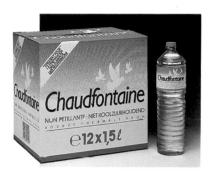

strategy is used to increase sales periodically by making people more aware of the product in its competitive environment, using means such as the pack of 12 bottles with its large display area.

3.3
THE BRAND AND ITS ATTRIBUTES

To complete the packaging strategy it is necessary to define the brand personality, the common denominator in communicating the brand image. A grid of opposite attributes is used to help the client put together an ideal character (old / young, serious / frivolous, traditional / modern, simple / complex, masculine / feminine, realist / dreamer). In the case of Chaudfontaine the characteristics were elegance, beauty, intelligence, charm, gentleness, youth, pride, calm, confidence and purety.

3.4
TALKING IMAGES

What does the image of the package say? That it is more concentrated, more absorbant, less fattening than the normal product? Or, at least, that the perception of its traditional or international character is improved, or that it is more readable, or part of a coherent range

with a strong family image? These diverse creative objectives determine the conceptual strategies to be used; for instance, a heraldic symbol conveys tradition, pastel colours are associated with femininity and lightness, a pictogram or symbol can portray essential product characteristics etc. For any objective a variety of visual concepts can be used, and it is up to the designer to use his creativity to both produce a large number of ideas and then to judge which are most appropriate. This section of the design request contains a list of all the graphic elements to be taken into consideration – logo, brand symbol, illustration, product and variety identification, promotional space, barcode etc, all of which have their place in a hierarchy of importance. Their place in the hierarchy varies according to the function and nature of the product, its reputation and the objectives of the manufacturer, in certain cases the brand name being most important and in others discretely used as a signature.

In the case of Chaudfontaine the logo is now in the centre of the label and the lightness of pure, fresh water is expressed by the doves in flight (recalling the original symbol), white on a soft background, as opposed to the stiff-looking bird used on the previous label, with the logo re-designed to express simple elegance.

3.5
IN TWO OR FOUR COLOURS

The final part of the briefing sets the technical, technological, linguistic and legal limitations, plus the printing method and number of colours available, all of which play a role in channeling creative thought. Obviously an image printed in four-colour separation will be very different from the same thing printed using two or three colours with no screen, although these technical limitations should be seen as a stimulus rather than a barrier to creativity. In the case of Rush, two-colour printing is used more effectively than the seven colours of the old label. The number of colours available is not the only thing to consider, merely the most visible, whereas the packaging material, format, text, number of languages and the deadline all have an influence on the type of printing techniques and materials used. With the exception of an inadequate budget and ridiculously short timing, technical limitations are not a barrier to creating a quality package as long as the design request is realistic and complete.

The Chaudfontaine label is printed in three colours using either a blue or red halftone background

depending on the variety to express softness and lightness, and the relatively limited technical means do not hinder the expression of the brand personality.

One cannot overemphasize the importance of the design request for the client and the designer as a way of grouping all the elements that must be considered, also because it contains the seeds of the solution to the problem. It is also necessary to identify elements that need to be tested, as when evaluated against objective criteria they enable a rational choice to be made. On the other hand, a bad briefing will never lead to a good package as the solutions provided will be in response to the objectives set out at the start of the project, reinforcing the importance of taking the time to put together a proper brief, and acting as a caution against incomplete or hasty briefings.

4.1
THE BRAND IS WORTH ITS WEIGHT IN GOLD

A brand is a combination of factors, historic, cultural and legal – with a life of its own transcending the product or its packaging, and evolving with time for as long as the product is a success. François Dalle, in the book *La Marque*,[15] states that a brand 'via its image sublimates the know-how of its country of origin... It is one of today's global realities. It is as much a part of consumer life as economic warfare between countries. It structures the relationships between different economic forces'. Also, 'A brand that does not renew its product dies: it loses its added value, the advantage of difference, its reason for being.' The brand is a key factor of modern business, constituting a form of capital, to the point that some companies count brand names as a capital asset in their annual report. Aggressive buy-outs of companies often conceal the fact that the real reason is to obtain the brand names rather than the company itself as the multinationals arm themselves to compete in the global market of tomorrow, using well-known brand names in the battle for market dominance. Well-known brands are not necessarily owned by big companies, but big companies invariably own famous brands knowing that in the public mind 'the brand is a public commitment to quality and performance'.[16] The brand is the stake in today's game of economic influence, and its creation, its perceived value and its protection are of incalculable importance.

4.2
THE CREATION OF A BRAND

When designing a package the brand name has special importance as the element that identifies it. J.N. Kapferer and G. Laurent assign it six functions: social expectations, purchasing pleasure, brand recall, reassurance, brand recognition, and product properties.[16] In packaging, identification and personality are fundamental and generally everything else follows. Major brands appropriate certain characteristics such as name, colour, symbol, shape or typography and use them as a visual base on which to build the other values associated with brand image such as international awareness. Its image in advertising, its strength against competition, and its cultural and image associations express the intrinsic quality of the product or the manufacturer's reputability. For an existing brand with a certain background it is important to check if the brand image works in the current visual environment, and with the aid of a well-prepared brand identity manual to check if it is being implemented in a disciplined and coherent fashion.

However, current visual environment does not mean following fashion, simply being sure that it is not out of context without losing sight of the value of the brand's historic associations. Examples of 'updating' a brand image are Koipe and Ciments d'Obourg, which show an evolution that brings the image into line with current market perceptions. It is necessary when updating a brand image to analyse its content, environment, personality, its visual conception as well as the brand strategy established in the brand identity manual.

THE BRAND AND ITS COMPONENTS

26

4.2.1
Content

With an existing brand, content becomes part of its history and therefore, when updating, it is necessary to be careful not to destroy the spirit or idea of the brand. In the case of Knorr the historic elements are the typestyle of the brand name and its red colour, plus the green and yellow colour combination associated with products that form the basis of the range.

The cultural content of a brand image deserves deeper psychoanalytic analysis, and will be the subject of a future work. The Flamenco dancer on Maya (Myrurgia) packaging in Spain, the Chinese flying horse, the Japanese Kirin and the Quaker on the US Quaker Oats packs go far beyond being brand symbols, having their origins in folklore, mythology or religion.

In the case of a new brand it is the name and the positioning of the product, often interrelated, that are the most important elements. 'The brand name can be the main expression of the brand's position: a well-chosen name can denote performance or benefit, efficiency or satisfaction. It can also help differentiate the product', which is the view of Jean-Marie Dru in *Le Saut Créatif*.[17] Mr Propre, Pampers and Luvs are all names related to the function or performance of the product. However it must be recognized that this

approach has limitations when used internationally (Mr Propre, Meister Proper, Mastro Lindo) and when translated lead to visual inconsistency in a multinational product or if not translated the significance of the name will be lost to most people. To understand the meaning of Pampers or Luvs you need to be an English speaker, whereas only a Swede would know that Gevalia's Ny Rost means 'New Roast'. This is

true of many brands both in the USA and Europe, supporting the idea that it is better to choose brand names without linguistic significance like Miaou, Omo, or Oë (deodorant).

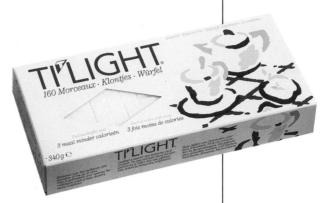

4.2.2
The world of
the brand

Each brand has its own world with a set of icons and symbols typical of its category. Beer, cigarettes, detergents, coffee, champagne or perfume, all have different visual environments each with its specific symbolism, but inexpensive own-brand products ignore these codes, calling into question their capacity for long-term survival. In many areas brands are so well-established that they are almost impossible to compete against as J. N. Kapferer observes in *La Marque*,[18] 'a generic brand name is only of value to a product when established manufacturers are either absent or quitting the market'. For new categories of products or for new varieties of existing products a new set of visual symbols is needed, as is the case with 'light' products, although whether a beer without alcohol or low-calorie sugar really belong with their predecessors is questionable when their main characteristics are so different. Ti'Light sugar from Tirlemont has three times fewer calories; Diet Coke and Mariana Light coffee fit into this new category (section 3.4). The danger is that if a new product does not integrate properly into its visual category, the brand will not be noticed and the consumer will be confused.

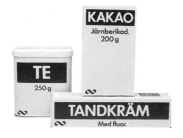

4.2.3
The brand personality

For many years Young & Rubicam have used an anthropomorphic approach to brand and product definition, a method that we have also applied to brand and package design in the belief that it helps the designer to have a better 'feeling' for the individual characteristics of a brand and is a better approach to finding ways to portray it.

Typestyle, colour, form and symbols all help give a brand 'individuality' and separate it from others. J.-P. Favre expresses it as 'the sum total of ideas, impressions, suggestions, prejudices and emotions which, in one way or another, stamp the personality of the product (the product image)'[19]; the product personality therefore perfectly expresses the manufacturer's 'business ideals'.

The adjectives used to establish the personality of Patek Philippe during the redesign of their corporate identity – 'skilled artisan, unconditionally in love with beauty, supplier to kings and princes' – say much more about the brand than company statistics. This is reflected in the design, which combines gold and silver, elegant typography and the Calatrava cross symbolizing nobility, a luxurious hallmark for a master watchmaker which not only fits in its environment, but also

stands out from competitors.

In *La Persuasion Clandestine* Vance Packard comments that 'the image of a living personality is much more difficult to imitate than the ingredients and quality of a product'.[20] Cartier, Yves Saint Laurent and Gucci all have a perfect understanding of the power of a prestige brand.

4.2.4
The concept

To stand out from the mass a brand must have something unique in order for people to notice it. Most major brands have a characteristic feature (e.g. the Gauloises helmet, the Mr Propre man, the Camel dromedary, the typestyle of the Kellogg's logo, the graphic structures of Pepsi Cola, Del Monte and Marlboro, the colours of Kodak, Ovomaltine (or Ovaltine) and Schweppes, all have this uniqueness). The ultimate goal is to make several memorable elements work together to form a single identity; the Gauloises helmet is associated with blue, the Knorr logo with a banner (section 4.2.1).

Choosing the final concept is not easy as generally there is more than one solution to a given problem and it is difficult to decide whether to use a symbol rather than a structure or colour. Generally a figurative symbol 'talks' and is more memorable than something abstract but with the

vast number of brands on the market it is becoming increasingly difficult to find something unique using only colour and typography. In the case of Ariel or Mr Propre, for example, the symbol is much more quickly identifiable than the logo.

4.2.5
Visual strategy

A company must first decide between using a company strategy or a brand strategy. Masaru Yoshimori calls them 'umbrella brands and multiple brands',[21] even though in some cases the two are linked in that the company name acts as a guarantee for the brand, with the brand indirectly implying the company's involvement. A company strategy is fairly straightforward (section 1.1) because any product, irrespective of category, carries the company image. Among many others Kodak and IBM are good examples of the company name aiding product identity. Brand strategy is altogether more complex to apply, being affected by the history, reputation and category of the products concerned, and being a function of the communication strategy, and the brand's positioning must be correctly applied in relation to the other graphic elements of the package. Each level of communication must be allotted a precise role in relation to the total package, with four levels being necessary to communicate a product definition: (i) the brand identity; (ii) the family; (iii) the variety and (iv) the sub-variety. Following this method a consumer should be able to understand and identify the product's characteristics versus others in the range and against competing brands. While it is not possible to establish a general rule, in most cases the logo represents the brand, the colour the family, the symbol the variety and a descriptive text the sub-variety. Often a sub-brand name is used (e.g. Danone's Danette, Dany and Danino) both to identify a variety or family and as a recollection of the

BRAND	LOGO	FORM, SYMBOL, COLOUR
FAMILY	COLOUR	SUFFIX, STRUCTURE, FORM OR MATERIAL
VARIETY	SYMBOL	TEXT, COLOUR, PHOTO
SUB-VARIETY	TEXT	COLOUR, SYMBOL

THE 4 LEVELS OF PRODUCT COMMUNICATION

main brand name; the Nutri-soja and Nutrimel brands of Nutricia use the same approach.

The visual elements used to identify each level can vary according to the problem.

An homogeneous family

There are product ranges with each product in the same category (e.g. Petit Navire with canned fish, Cepsa with motor oil or Milka with chocolate products). The brand image is dominant, with the variety a secondary element, even when, as is the case with Petit Navire, there are sub-families and sub-brands as with Milka. The size of the brand identity depends on the relative value of the

other elements. Tirlemont sugars prefer to show the product and place the 'T' symbol as a signature in the top left corner of their packaging.

Several parallel families

Line extensions, whether a different form of the same product (liquid, concentrated liquid) or the use of an existing name in another category (perfume using the brand name of a ball-point pen manufacturer) have

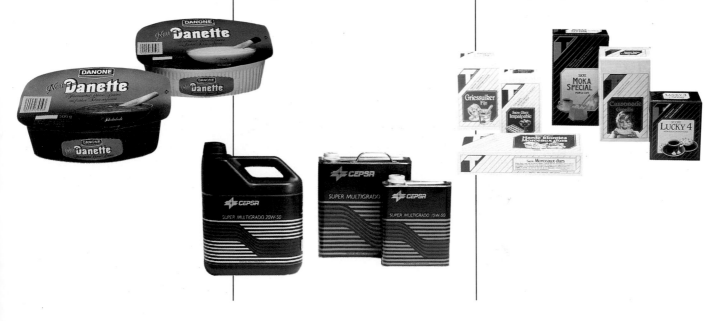

become a fact of everyday life due to the cost of creating and launching a new brand. It is less costly to take an established brand and build on its reputation – like Gauloises with light, extra light and then Gauloises Blondes, a type of cigarette totally different to everything the brand had been associated with, and proving the persuasive power of a well-known brand name. However, in their book *Le Marketing Guerrier*,[22] Al Ries and Jack Trout maintain

that 'although line extensions almost always succeed in the short term, as for example Miller Lite and Diet Coke, in the long term the product will fail'.

The varieties of Coca-Cola (section 4.2.2) and Ariel are examples of this policy. The problem with this type of approach is to retain the visual integrity of the brand image and not to dilute the most important brand characteristics. Does Coca-Cola without sugar, or a 'nectar'

version of a fruit juice help support the quality image of the basic product? A more convincing way of moving into another category was that used by Granini who developed an additional fruit juice range under the name Primus.

The manufacturer's signature

Only if it adds to the quality impression of a product is it worth adding the manufacturer's logo or symbol; it is difficult to imagine Nestlé using their name on cosmetics. It is of course their food products such as Nescafé, Nesquik and Cérélac that benefit from this association. Large multinationals like Monsanto, Johnson Wax and Nabisco/Belin all use this approach, in contrast to Unilever and Procter & Gamble with their wide variety of products including many different categories. It is difficult to define with certainty the limits of the power of a brand, as they exist for the most part in the consumer's mind even before the manufacturer is aware of them. A brand cannot necessarily be used in every area of new product and new range development.

4.2.6
The brand identity manual

As with a corporate identity manual, a brand identity manual sets out guidelines showing how to use the visual components of the brand, and is vital in maintaining the visual integrity of the brand when applied in different situations over a period of time.

The main brand characteristics are defined in terms of graphic construction, symbol, structure, typography and colour with illustrations of the main applications. Anyone using the brand identity should follow the guidelines scrupulously.

A major brand has a difficult life, and it can die through lack of visual continuity; therefore, it should stay visually cohesive whatever the application. The brand identity manual exists to ensure this, and the adjacent examples show extracts from Knorr and Dextro Energy (CPC).

As we have seen, the brand name is the focal point of the package and its design or updating should precede any package design work. The brand strategy dictates the design of the package and is one of the most important aspects of product communication.

Knowing that the packaging strategy is influenced by the market situation the manufacturer will wish to position his product on the best possible selling platform, i.e. to attract, inform, convince and satisfy consumers on a long-term basis, which means better communication of the characteristics and promise of the product. This leads to the examination of the stages necessary in a 'rational' package design study. Creativity is not at odds with business objectives, but it must be applied in a disciplined way, which is why I have adopted for myself Leonardo da Vinci's saying that 'art is born of constraint and dies of liberty'.

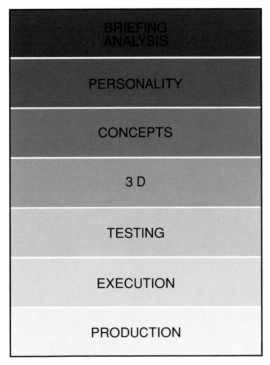

BRIEFING ANALYSIS

PERSONALITY

CONCEPTS

3 D

TESTING

EXECUTION

PRODUCTION

THE CREATIVE PROCESS

5.1 DEFINING THE PROBLEM

Using the briefing (dealt with in Chapter 3) as a basis, the commercial analysis enables the designer to familiarize himself with the market situation and the main competitors by evaluating the strengths and weaknesses of the product versus others in the same area. This is done in the shop or by entering packages into a computer and creating simulated mass displays enabling a profile of each product to be prepared as a function of the criteria established in the personality grid (sympathetic, innovative, experienced etc.). This qualitative analysis translates into the packaging strategy, bearing in mind the communication strategy mentioned in the previous chapter. The use of different 'problem-solving' methods helps to refine and evaluate these strategies by working as a group, the resulting analysis allowing the product personality to be defined.

5.2 DISCOVERING THE PERSONALITY

Mr Knorr is a talented chef. He demands top quality. He is popular, likeable and friendly. He uses his know-how and creativity to prepare original top-quality recipes. He masters modern technology and is a recognized authority. His main professional objective is to offer clients exclusive dishes that are delicious either to eat alone or in company.

This personality illustrates the way in which we see the personality of a brand or package, being the ideal character that the client would wish his product to have, and which the consumer should perceive. This type of anthropomorphic portrait illustrates the 'collection of ideas, attitudes, attributes or qualities' that can be communicated to the consumer via the brand and its special envoy: the package.

Starting as a text, the personality is translated into visual terms to give the package a unique and personal identity. It is the basis of the briefing, and using adjectives comprises the list of attributes enabling the designer or the client to evaluate possible solutions.

5.3
FINDING IDEAS

The best approach to creating visual concepts is the alternation of individual work and group work (brainstorming), the group often sparking off new directions while staying within the constraints of the briefing, and leading to maximum output of creativity. To achieve this, a

designer uses traditional methods, or graphic computers as well as the elements of visual language: form, texture, structure, colour, type and images (photo, symbol, illustration). These elements are examined more closely in Chapter 6.

The way in which the main brand attributes are treated visually should never detract from the key objectives of positioning the product, explaining it and convincing the consumer, not forgetting the specific design objectives set down in the briefing. Having said this, it remains true that a package is part of everyday life and the product must be bought in preference to competing items, needing to arouse sympathy by its beauty, style and unity. Not only does 'ugliness not sell' as Raymond Loewy said, but also consumer goods can play a role in creating a new form of modern aesthetics.

5.4
SEE IN THREE
DIMENSIONS

Form and shape are inseparable from packaging and for this reason any promising solution should be adapted into three-dimensional form. Each face of a package needs to be properly structured to integrate the necessary elements (legal mentions, text, illustrations) so that they can fulfil their requirements properly and remain visually in harmony with the rest of the package. These final mock-ups are just like the real thing and are important both for the designer and for the client because in packaging no detail is unimportant, and all contribute to the overall perception of quality. At this stage in development, before spending a lot of money on preparing mock-ups, it is better to use computer simulations as an aid to looking at how different designs work in three dimensions, and to compare them to the competition. A package does not exist in isolation and the only realistic way to evaluate it is in its commercial environment, whether actual or by computer simulation.

5.5
BE UNDERSTOOD

Nowadays it would be extremely dangerous to launch a new product without first consumer testing it to verify that the brand personality is properly perceived and appreciated by the consumer, and given the cost of a new product launch, it is essential to limit the potential for error.

Testing has its own dangers if the correct questions are not asked or the consumer is requested to design the package or the proper testing procedure is not used. Why ask someone without specialized knowledge what they think of a colour, the subtlety of typography, the value of a symbol or illustration when what you want to know is whether the design communicates the main brand characteristics and personality? This is why a method was created that is qualitative but quick and easy to use in order to determine how well design proposals convey the desired personality profile.

A limited sample of people (+/- 100) which is representative of the market is more than adequate to verify whether or not a design is on target (section 5.1). Qualitative testing helps the marketing department to select the best solution, but should not replace judgement and initiative as testing is only an aid, although a valuable one in decision-making.

5.6
REFINE THE EXECUTION

This last stage in the development of a package is most important and is dealt with in greater detail in Chapter 8.

The quality of artwork supplied to the engraver has repercussions on the quality of the final package and the designer should be involved throughout the process. A badly-printed package can destroy all or part of the creative effort that was put in, emphasizing the need to spend the time and money to see that it is done properly. Artwork is not secondary to design, and should not be considered inferior.

The choice of typeface, layout, photography and illustration, and the choice of colour are all elements that need careful co-ordination to be executed properly, as do engraving, printing and manufacture. Precision and control are the watchwords. Precision in the methods and equipment used (e.g. the graphic computer) and control to ensure that the design is respected and suitable for production often lead to savings in production costs, or increased functionality (Chapter 2).

These are the important stages in a properly executed design study, showing how rational creativity applied in a disciplined way can lead to a package that is persuasive, aesthetic and efficiently communicates the brand identity.

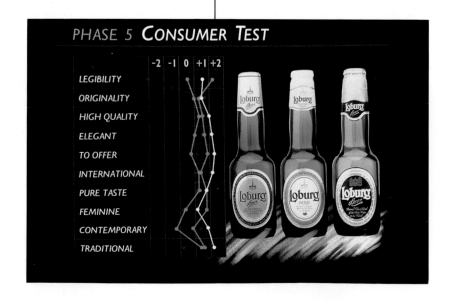

PHASE 5 CONSUMER TEST

	-2	-1	0	+1	+2
LEGIBILITY					
ORIGINALITY					
HIGH QUALITY					
ELEGANT					
TO OFFER					
INTERNATIONAL					
PURE TASTE					
FEMININE					
CONTEMPORARY					
TRADITIONAL					

This chapter sets out not only to sing the praises of our business, but also to emphasize the aesthetic importance of packaging, not merely as something mass-produced, but as part of our culture.

The *Bauhaus* gave great importance to incorporating aesthetics in all spheres of human activity and Georges Patrix in 'Beauté et Laideur'[23] remarked that 'the aesthetic is a message superior to function, and gives rise to spontaneous enthusiasm bringing joy to the individual or society who benefits from it. It is no longer sales talk or a demonstration that leads to purchase, it is the face of the product that must win over the client. This "face" is its aesthetic value'. This 'face' is the package itself.

This chapter describes the main elements of visual language used by a designer to convey his message, a language rich and full of nuance, form and function, symbols, brand, colour, typography, image, graphic structure, material and texture.

Any attempt to dissect the components of a package destroys the whole and it goes without saying that a package is the result of a judicious mix of elements, an entity which expresses, in a unique and individual way, the brand identity. On the other hand, each element can work on different levels giving a multifaceted richness to the mix, and certain brands have had the good fortune or intelligence to appropriate some of them, giving them a certain exclusiveness.

Lighting and instore placement are two factors outside the designer's control, and although these are important elements they are at the mercy of the distributor. A carton in a badly-lit situation or stacked on the floor is at a disadvantage, a situation which a package that is simple, clearly understandable and visible can do something to overcome. Each of these elements of the visual vocabulary can in its turn help in communicating the brand message, the product, its function or the way information is transmitted. These four levels constitute the structure of the following analysis.

6.1
THE ELEMENTS OF A
VISUAL LANGUAGE

6.1.1
Form

In packaging, form has a rather special role to play, particularly when such things as liquids, creams, powders or granules rely on their packaging to give them a shape. The form can identify the brand, the product or its function, and standardization imposed by distributors or, because of the packing machinery used, limits the opportunities to give a product uniqueness. This must be compensated for in other elements of the packaging mix.

The way colour is used can change perception of form and as Favre comments, 'The same colour, with a rounded shape or a jagged one, does not produce at all the same effect. A soft and pleasing colour harmony can compensate the austere lines of a design'.[24]

Shape adds personality

Perrier or Coca-Cola bottles identify the brand instantly and are at least as, if not more important than the graphics and colours associated with the brand. Granini, Heinz Ketchup and Bière des Druides are other examples where form plays a major role in identifying the brand whereas the trend is towards sameness and standardization. A series of technical factors dictate what

the form will be (i.e. production, filling, distribution, display etc.), none of which help when trying to create something different. The Loburg beer bottle is a good example of what can be achieved in providing uniqueness, especially when you are aware of the limitations imposed by mass production of bottles and the filling line. Sylphide and Boursault are examples from the cheese area; Côte d'Or uses a traditional 'toffee wrapper' around the chocolate box

giving the product individuality and recalling toffee.

The shape is the product

Shape often describes the product category (e.g. a champagne bottle, a cigarette carton, a Tetra Brik pack of milk or fruit juice, a yoghurt pot or a jam jar). Form provides the common denominator for the entire category, playing no role in distinguishing one product from another, except for d'Aucy, who completely

rethought the shape of the traditional metal can.

Sometimes the type of product plays a more specific role in influencing the design of the package form as in the case of Epi d'Or maize oil which reflects the shape of a corn cob, or Looza and Orangina fruit bottles which use a citrus fruit texture. The 'cook book' packages for Yarden pre-prepared meals are an especially original way of associating the product with the package.

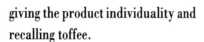

The functional shape

The importance of function was briefly reviewed in Chapter 2, being an element that can influence the design of the package form, as exemplified by the Jacqmotte coffee filter, where form and product are inseparable. A liquid wax shoe polish applicator has its own unique shape as does W.C. Canard (Toilet Duck) by Johnson Wax which uses the U-bend of the toilet as its motif.

The way the product is used often determines the form of the package (e.g. Ariel and its dosing ball, and the Shell oil can – Puissance 5 – with a flexible spout), as well as many products with handles and other features that make usage simpler.

In the case of re-usable packages, packages that become toys or that double as a tool, it is often difficult to distinguish which is the package and which is the product.

Examples of packages that are both practical and functional include Monsavon (sold in a shaving bowl), the Canderel and Gillette distributors, the Los Hermanos (Burgundy by the glass system) where the bottle is supplied with a glass and the Marie Brizard bottle which also serves as a shaker; the coffee in spray form launched in Japan is a new way of serving coffee.

6.1.2
The material
Material, form and colour are inseparable and it can be said that the material gives the form its identity. As an example, imagine the same form, opaque or transparent, or in plastic or glass and you can see that they are not the same thing and although colour is discussed below, it affects form in that a light colour gives an impression of a larger size than a dark one.

The material becomes part of the brand

Each type of material has its own unique characteristics, properties that can either influence or change the personality of the brand. Glass, with its sterility and transparency, can readily be linked to purity and prestige; plastic is perfect where functionalism and ease of use are concerned; it would be practical to use metal, a cold, hard material, in situations where lightness and freshness are required, whereas carton board is a perfect material when you need to print an illustration or photo.

Aside from its characteristic shape, it would be difficult to imagine producing a champagne bottle in anything other than glass, so strong is the association with the product, and perhaps the best example of this kind of association is the green, satin-finished Remy Martin cognac bottle.

Each type of material has an identity and a creative mind can use this advantageously to reinforce the personality of the product, glass becoming utilitarian and corrugated card a luxury item (section 6.1.7).

Each product has its material

Materials tend to be associated with particular product categories: glass being used for preserves, beer, wine, spirits, perfume and pharmaceuticals (except when easy use is a priority and ring-pull cans or wine boxes are used). Metal is used mainly for preserves, drinks and oil cans, aerosols and closures; plastics for foods (cheeses, yoghurt, oils, table waters), detergents, cosmetics and chemical products, whereas carton board and its composite derivatives (aluminium, card, plastic, laminates) are used for mass consumption items like foods, detergents and cosmetics. However, given the currently increasing preoccupation with ecology, the coming years will see some revolutionary changes in the way materials are used (Chapter 2).

Materials as an aid to function

Card is printable, plastic is light and mouldable, metal is rigid, glass is transparent, lightweight glass is recyclable – all properties that influence how a package functions. The material/function relationship is of fundamental importance when improving the functionalism of a package; lightweight glass for non-returnable bottles, the printability and ease-of-use card-aluminium-plastic laminate Tetra Brik packs, and semi-rigid bottles for cosmetics all illustrate the direct relationship between material and function. The role of packaging materials in protecting and preserving products is explained in detail in *Le Pack*[25] as well as in *Packaging*[26] (Design in Motion).

6.1.3
Colour

Along with form, colour is the other element fundamental to packaging. The Gauloises blue, Kodak yellow, Milka's mauve, and the pink of Oil of Olaz (or Oil of Ulay) and Mon Chéri all illustrate how colour can be the dominant element of a brand identity. Colour is a complex area because of its symbolic and cultural associations, its dependance on light conditions and the fact that it can never be seen in isolation. As G. Patrix commented 'a colour on its own could be beautiful, but we never see one colour, always *groups* of colour'.[27] This is important since a colour out of context does not function, as without a colour next to it it has no optical effect such as when a blue is placed next to red it looks warmer than when next to green.

Colour as a symbol

The ambivalence common to symbols is also true of colour, as they can be positive or negative, warm or cold (e.g. red and green, with green being fertile, receptive and cool and red active, mobile and warm). Curiously enough, 'blood red is the complementary colour of vegetable green, and when mixed makes white, the colour of sunlight', this being the way in which R.L. Rousseau introduces the symbolism of colour in his book *Le Langage des Couleurs.*[28]

Colour symbolism is a vast subject, but for the sake of simplicity this discussion will be confined to considering some of the symbolism associated with the basic colours (red, yellow, green, blue, white, black), not forgetting that colour cannot exist in isolation, and that it requires the right background to be able to stand out.

♦ Red: symbol of activity, wine, fire, warmth, the heart, love, masculinity, power, etc., also danger, burning, passion, drama and war.

♦ Yellow: colour of light and sunlight, the colour of gold, warmth, energy and joy, golden harvests, butter, honey and vegetable oil; yellow can also portray the deadly heat of the desert, treason and sickness.

♦ Green: colour of fertility, passivity, water, the moon, femininity, spring, the resurrection and hope; also the symbol of putrefaction, reptiles and poison.

♦ Blue: fresh, feminine, the colour of the sky and the air, associated with spirituality and wisdom, passiveness, the horizon and deep calm; also associated with the idea of death.

♦ Black: the colour of night and death, black is the absence of colour, a void; like night and day, black is linked to white, symbolizing binary rhythms, light and dark; also the colour of solemnity.

♦ White: the fusion of colours that form light; white symbolizes purity, virginity, infinity, and is associated

with silver as yellow is with gold; in the East white is the colour of death. Black and white are binary and can be combined with warm or cold colours to convey masculinity or femininity, active or passive.

Although this is only a brief overview it should be enough to give an idea of how complex the subconscious aspects of colour are.

Colour and the brand

P. Zelanski and M.P. Fisher give a resumé of the psychological role that colour plays in packaging.[29] 'A survey of packaging design reveals that yellow, red and orange are often effectively used to draw attention, purple is frequently associated with luxury products, blue suggests cleanliness and/or quietness, and green evokes an impression of nature. Gold, silver and black effectively promise high quality merchandise'. The association of Coca-Cola and Marlboro with red, Gauloises and Ducados with blue is obvious, but it takes more than just colour to create an identity, the brand name and/or symbol is necessary to make it work.

When colour acts as 'signal' for a brand it gives it much more visibility in its sales environment and a big competitive advantage, even if the dominant colour makes it more difficult to identify other varieties in the same range. The mauve of the Milka range (section 4.2.5) and the

blue of Nivea are irreplaceable because of their role in identifying the brand.

Tell me product, what is your colour?
Colour works on different levels, either identifying what the product is – white for unbranded products or light products, brown for chocolate – or to distinguish varieties within a certain range. In the first situation it is associated with the nature of the product (as with white for detergent) whereas in the second it becomes part of a code that helps identify varieties within a product family.

At this point it begins to become more complex because identifying a variety can start to interfere with identifying product differences within a range: light, without sugar, no calories, etc. and in this type of case colour may not be enough to make the difference clear. A combination of colour, graphic structure, visuals and text should achieve this (section 4.2.5). Contrary to the view expressed by Favre,[30] colours aren't necessarily linked to a particular

product. If this were the case all chocolate packages would be brown and look rather similar.

A colour for every function
In their book *Dictionnaire des Symboles*,[31] J. Chevalier and A. Gheerbrant describe the symbolic function of colour as follows. 'The first characteristic of colour symbolism is its universal nature, not just geographic, but at all levels of being and of cosmic, psychological and mystic knowledge.' Psychologists make a distinction between warm and cold colours, the first aiding the process of adaptation and involvement (red, orange, yellow) – they have the power to stimulate and excite, and the second group have the opposite effect (blue, indigo, violet) having a calming, sedative influence.

The symbolic function of colour discussed above is generally subconscious and even hidden within the context of the package, as generally only the physical and psychological functions are obvious (see section 6.1.3). The physical function makes a package stand out from its competition, not just by using a colour to identify it, but by on-shelf repetition creating a large and highly-visible mass of colour, an important factor in giving a product 'presence'.

Colour plays its psychological role by transferring the associations it has with the package: warm, aggressive, masculine red; calm, cold, feminine blue; glowing, intuitive, happy yellow; fertile, spring-like, cool green. Colour can make a package richer, warmer or colder, more masculine or feminine, more calm or more natural. On this basis Gauloises is calm, Marlboro aggressive. Colour can also describe product function as is the case with Pampers which uses a blue package for boys and a pink package for girls (section 4.2.1).

Colour explains

Any colour that forms part of a code identifying the product or its usage can be considered informative. In Switzerland Maryland tobacco is identified by the colour yellow, the code for filter or light being much less important, showing that for the Swiss, the type of tobacco is considered to be the most important part of the message to the point where Gauloises had to change its traditional colour. In Belgium carbonated and non-carbonated mineral waters are identified by the colours red and blue; and white, or rather the absence of colour signifies products that are cheap as opposed to known brands. Colour can also inform about the nature of a product (i.e. a black cross on an orange background warns of dangerous chemicals, the orange skull of poisons, and there is the yellow and black radiation symbol).

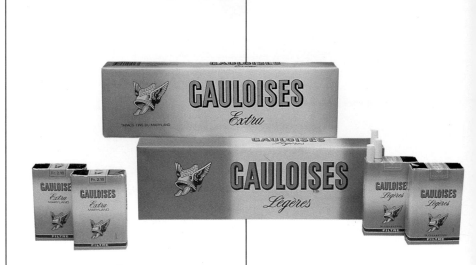

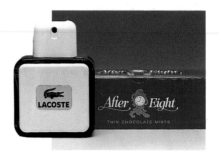

6.1.4
The symbol

After form, material and colour, the three physical elements of visual language, the symbol is the main 'graphic' element in an identity; its ability to provoke recall and its visual qualities make it the focal point in brand communication, especially on an international level. Symbols are universal, and without using language can convey a fairly complex message – 'A picture is worth a thousand words', states the old cliché. Like colour, a symbol can have hidden meaning: completeness, femininity, the softness of a circle, symmetry, masculinity, the rigidity of a square, the aggressiveness of a triangle (point in the air) or its receptivity (point downwards), the dynamism of a cross etc. At the end of the chapter the interelationships between colour, form, symbols and the other elements of visual language are explained graphically in the form of a 'syntactic cross'.

The symbol is often the brand
The Gauloises helmet, the Mr Propre man, the Camel dromedary, the Marlboro triangle, and the Coca-Cola wave are all brand symbols capable of communicating what the brand is completely on their own. A good symbol, whether figurative or abstract, can stand alone if it is distinctive and memorable, and is probably more important than the

logo when it successfully expresses the brand personality. The Pampers baby crosses language barriers more easily than any other element of the identity, as do the Lacoste crocodile, the After Eight clock, the Iglo fork, the Uncle Ben's head, the Sandeman, Johnnie Walker, and Beefeater characters, the Vache qui rit cow's head, the effigies of L'Alsacienne and Dr Oetker.

A symbol can contain different

levels and meanings and is therefore an especially efficient communication tool. In evaluating the semiotic value of signs and symbols, U. Eco says that 'they are unequivocal, equivocal, pluri-vocal or symbolic',[32] that is to say that except for unequivocal symbols, they have different shades of meaning and content. The Camel symbol is obviously associated with the cigarette, but has secondary associations with

warmth, sun, desert, the exotic and adventure. Except in Muslim countries, the red cross signifies medicine; the green cross means pharmacy in the West and security in Japan. In Belgium the blue cross is the symbol of an organization that rescues abandoned animals, and is an international symbol for animal welfare. In this example the symbol remains the same, but the colour modifies its meaning.

Symbolizing the product

In addition to the many ideograms that are seen every day in stations, airports and on the highway, 'signs' can identify a product or its category: goat's milk cheese is often signified by a goat's head. Vegetable oils and margarines are generally identified by symbolizing the plant from which they are derived: maize, sunflower, ground nuts, olive etc; meat stock cubes by the animal; jams, fruit juices and shampoos by the fruit. All of these signs are much clearer than using text to explain the product.

The symbol identifies function

In the detergent world, a washing machine symbol communicates that the product is for machine use rather than handwash (e.g. the '3' in the Dash 3 logo denotes the product's triple action). On frozen products the stars clearly indicate storage life, and the belt and bow symbols that are used in addition to the background colour of Pampers indicate if they are for boys or girls (see 'A colour for every function', section 6.1.3).

Symbols explain more quickly

On international multilingual packaging, symbols can be an excellent way of replacing text, especially in the usage, dosage, temperature or contents messages. On Pampers packages there are ten languages so clear usage illustrations are used to explain how to utilize the product; this is often also the case with cleaning products.

Typography

In *The Gütenberg Galaxy*, M. McLuhan says that 'Typography is not only technology ... it is a packaged information, a portable commodity – typographic man has a new sense of time: cinematic, sequential and pictorial'.[33] Each typeface has a character of its own: the femininity of a roman italic, the virility of a gothic bold, the elegance of Garamond, the calm seriousness of Helvetica, the traditional air of Times can be marvellous aids in expressing brand personality. Michael Beaumont defines good typography as follows: 'Good typography is to do with shape, balance and colour. Always be aware of the shape your type makes – it is always important to consider not just the shape that the individual characters or words create, but the spaces around and within those actual shapes'.[34]

Typography is the brand personality

The main elements in any brand identity are the colour, symbol and type-style of the brand name, but in some instances typography must play this important role unaided. Having seen the importance of the brand and despite the success of certain 'generic' and unbranded products, I remain convinced that a product without a brand does not exist as it has no sense of being, either in time or in a spatial context.

These products have no 'typographic identity', the mark or signature that is proof of origin and quality with enough individuality to enable consumers to identify them from competitive products.

Carlsberg, Lu, Camel, Bayer, Maizena and Hero all use highly distinctive type-styles for their logos and none could be confused with any other brand in the same market sector.

It is very difficult to design a new logo, as it involves more than just using a typeface. Even if a typestyle is the original inspiration for the design, a designer must use texture, distortion, outline, drop shadow, colour etc, to give the logo a unique personality. Putting the logo within a shape is another way to add originality, as in the case of Danone, Kraft and Lipton.

Typography reflects the type of product

The product personality helps when choosing a typeface for product and variety definition, and though legibility is an important factor, it must not be compromised in the search for originality. 'Much of the art of choosing the correct typeface and weight lies in the combination of product association with the designer's aesthetic judgement. For example, to promote jewellery, a designer would consider a choice of delicate forms, probably a fine serif

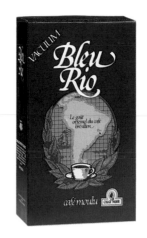

or an italic'.[35] Patek Philippe is a good illustration of this, Milka beautifully expresses milkiness, and Kronenbourg the Gothic personality of beer; the feeling of ice and cold is instantly evoked by the type-style of the Miko ice-cream logo.

Typography applies to all written information

The typography of a package isn't just the brand name or product description, but all of the text necessary to communicate the relevant information to the consumer, whether it be product characteristics, composition (including additives), usage method or category, as well as incorporating technical and legal mentions; plus, in a European or worldwide context all this is done in a number of different languages, usually being divided by cultural area (Asia, Northern Europe, Southern Europe, USA, Africa).

The visual structuring of a multilingual package is never easy. It requires clarity of typography and layout allied to good readability, with care taken not to use a typeface too small to be properly printed. Nothing is worse to the consumer than an incorrect or clumsy translation – the more reason, whenever possible, to use ideograms or pictograms instead of text, as they are much more quickly understood (see 'Symbols explain more quickly', section 6.1.4).

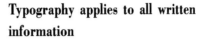

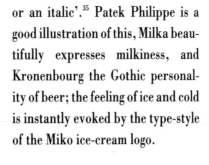

6.1.6
Images

Images, be they graphic, photographic, stylized, abstract or symbolic, can evoke practically anything, and often constitute the essential elements behind visual strategies used in packaging. They are used to express origin, tradition, usage and content (e.g. the Bleu Rio coffee illustration shows its origin, Ti'Light expresses lightness (section 4.2.2), Chambourcy its content, whereas Wilson's products and Japanese tea packages beautifully suggest tradition).

However, even the most seductive image is not enough to constitute a good package, as a pack is neither a poster nor an ad. It needs its own individual graphic structure to create a unique brand character. In some cases the use of an image may actually be detrimental to the product concept, as in the case of 'generic' products, most pharmaceuticals and certain prestige products.

The evocative power of imagery

The boat on the Petit Navire package and the Pampers baby are both used to identify the brand (section 4.2.5). In the case of Petit Navire the image and its structure are the central elements, whereas Pampers uses an omega shape around the baby illustration to give it uniqueness – a key identifying element for

the brand. In the same way, the shape of the label for Oil of Olaz (or Oil of Ulay) (section 6.1.3), the Marlboro triangle (see 'Colour and the brand', section 6.1.3) and the Heinz keystone (see 'Shape adds personality', section 6.1.1) are graphic elements that identify the brand. Heraldry holds a special place in packaging and anyone interested should read *Heraldic Design* by Heather Child.[36] Heraldry is a language unto itself and is used in cigarette packaging, beers, liqueurs, apéritifs and any type of traditional or prestige product to imply tradition and *savoir-faire* and with it the quality associated with certain origins. Chivas Regal, Dunhill and Jacksons of Piccadilly are eloquent users of this approach, and as V. Packard said in *La Persuasion Clandestine*, 'Packaging can sell the feeling of having roots'.[37]

The image tells a story

For frozen foods, ready-to-serve foods, preserves, jams, canned fish and certain drinks, it is the image, whether photographic or illustrative, that relates most of the product story, helping to tempt the consumer. Findus and Miau packaging are representative of this huge area. On the other hand, the Henkell Trocken bubbles are evoking the sparkling of champagne as well as festive confetti.

Packaging such as that for Bleu Rio (see section 6.1.6) or Nescafé instant coffee, or Evian mineral water use imagery to show the product's origin, employing tradition and the pre-supposed know-how that accompanies it, which is justifiable as long as it is true. This is certainly the case with beers (such as Heineken, Mahou, Kronenbourg); coffees (such as Jacqmotte and Douwe Egberts); Godiva chocolates and Amora mustard; all of these

products have a long tradition in their respective areas. Some manufacturers use a contrived 'old-fashioned' look to give their products the appearance of being hand-crafted or traditional and we should be careful not to confuse an old-fashioned look with one that is traditional. Each period has its own visual language and style but it is perfectly possible to express tradition using a current visual language (e.g. Saimaza and Stella Artois). It is tempting to follow fashion even though a 'Retro'-style package (1920s, 1950s ...) will last only as long as the trend does. A package should be in tune with its time without using elements from the dictates of current fashion.

A picture is quicker than text
As well as explaining the different varieties, imagery conveys the flavour, the smell or the specific

nature of a particular version of the product. There are many examples of this approach (the Chambourcy fruit cocktails, products with fruit scent or flavour such as detergents or an air-freshner with lemon, the ingredients of the Nadler Snack Bar range, the plants used to make deodorant essences for the Brise range, and generally any image that 'explains' the product).

6.1.7
Texture

Texture is part of the form and the material of the package and can be used to add an extra dimension to the appearance of the product, helping position it or to explain its function. Die-cut carton, embossed metal, flint or textured glass, and marbled plastic all have a feeling of texture, which can add a 'tactile' appearance to a package which, if well executed, makes it more pleasant to handle. Texture can also be used to provide better grip on the product.

Texture is like a skin
Texture can heighten certain aspects of a product – obvious with Kenzo or Guerlain perfumes or the embossed label of Faberge's Brut, all luxury, prestige products. The texture of the Perwoll bottle conveys the suppleness of fabric and the softness of wool; that of Granini and Looza the texture of citrus fruit; and the Epi

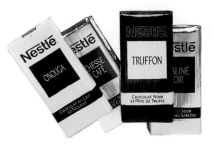

d'Or maize oil bottle has the form of a corn cob (see 'Shape adds personality' and 'The shape is the product', section 6.1.1). The simplicity and embossing of the Nestlé chocolate labels give their products a much higher-quality impression than traditional chocolate packs.

Texture packages better

Texture, as used on most plastic vegetable oil and mineral water bottles, has the dual function of adding rigidity while increasing grip (e.g. Vandemoortele), this is also true of the majority of screw-caps and shower products (Tahiti).

6.2 VISUAL SYNTAX

Syntax and grammar are used to organize the elements of a phrase, and one can attempt to create a visual syntax by combining the different components that have been analysed above. Theoreticians disagree with the respective order of colours in the colour wheel. 'Goethe and Alfred Hödzel begin with red because it is the most intense colour; Klee chooses violet-red, as it is formed by a union of the two extreme colours of the spectrum; the Swiss colour theorist Johannes Itten places yellow at the top of the wheel, since it is the brightest colour and the closest to white light'.[38]

Opposites of green/blue–red/yellow are most logical because they go from cold to warm, the active vertical and passive horizontal, merging to form a cross (the symbol of unity) combining the spectrum in its centre to form white light. If the main character traits of 'Le Senne'[39] are superimposed on this colour wheel, interesting and sometimes surprising relationships between a personality and its visual components (symbols, typography, form, material) can be established. Using this method it is discovered that the Marlboro package is masculine, warm, active and extrovert because it uses red as the dominant colour and a triangle with its apex pointing

upwards (see 'Colour and the brand', section 6.1.3).

The relationship beween form and colour is well-expressed by Favre.[40] 'Blue gives the impression of disappearing from our sight in a concentric movement and is best suited to the circle. Red is also in movement but this is neither concentric nor eccentric. It is a movement for itself without radiation, which teams up excellently with the square. The triangle corresponds best to the eccentric movement of yellow. The use of a shape which does not conform to the colour, intentionally or not, produces accentuated or diminished effects.'

It is possible to make a brand feminine or masculine, active or passive or to combine two complementary facets (i.e. when an active colour such as red is rendered less active by using it in a circular shape). Conversely, a passive colour can become more 'aggressive' when used as a square shape. U. Eco refers to this as a 'double-jointed' code.[41] The Bass identity is masculine with its red triangle but its typography is feminine. A blue square becomes feminine and sensitive because of its colour, although a square is essentially masculine and any symbol is capable of expressing opposite aspects of the same personality, as for instance in the way that Gauloises uses blue to soften the essentially warlike character of the

helmet (section 4.2.4). The Pepsi Cola symbol, which is essentially a feminine shape, is made more active by using red in the same way that the Lucky Strike circle is feminine by shape, masculine by colour.

The personalities shown in the diagram can obviously be replaced by more up-to-date examples (i.e. the extrovert or passionate could become a young Turk, the realist a US 'achiever', the stable, the conservative or the indifferent and the imaginative, the creative or the dreamer). J.-M. Dru emphasizes the need to concentrate on broad trends when analysing lifestyles.[42] Psychological research confirms the main colour-to-character relationships: 'Extroverts tend to prefer warm hues; introverts like cool hues. Red is usually the preference of vibrant, ongoing, impulsive people'.[43]

As all personalities are complex by nature, it is rare to discover or to be able to create a homogenous group of signs; this is the case with the Gitanes package where all three elements of the brand (colour, the gypsy symbol and the type) contribute to a totally feminine personality, as with Perrier which uses a round form in association with the feminine colour of green (see 'Shape adds personality', section 6.1.1).

Typography can also contribute to building up the psychological character: English Script suits an emotive/non-active one; Futura an

active/emotive one; Baskerville a non-active/non-emotive one; Rockwell an active/non-emotive one.

The 'syntactic cross' becomes more profound with the addition of the symbolism associated with iron, gold, copper and tin, and the four traditional symbolic elements – fire, earth, water, air; or cultural characteristics such as heritage, tradition, *savoir-faire*, culture. In this respect it is interesting to observe that Mr Propre is on a yellow background surrounded by a green halo (water) as he is masculine and active, the know-how champion (the good genie).

The 'syntactic cross' should not be thought of as a miracle solution, but rather as an especially revealing aid to thought and brand personality research!

THE SYNTACTIC CROSS

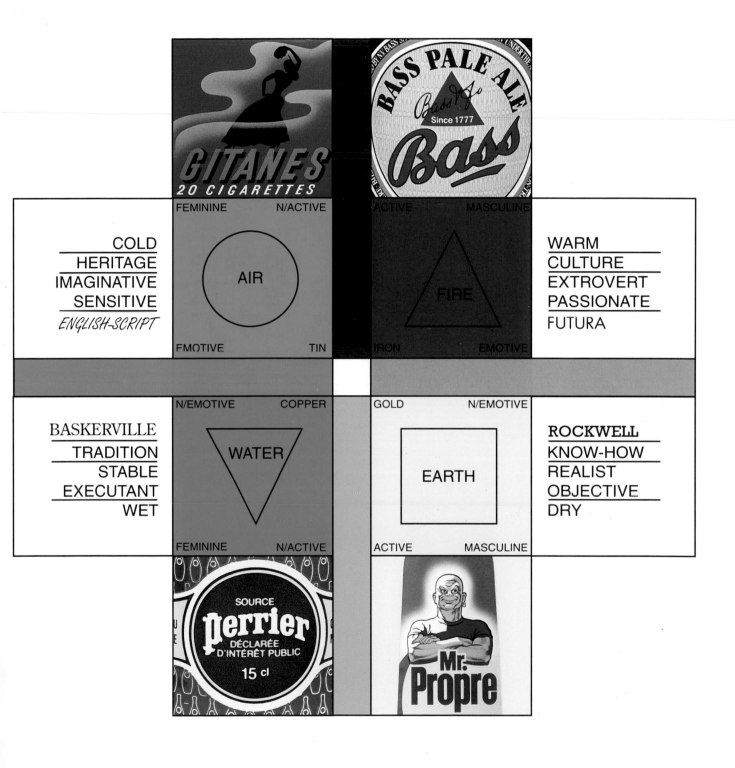

FEMININE   N/ACTIVE   ACTIVE   MASCULINE

COLD
HERITAGE
IMAGINATIVE
SENSITIVE
ENGLISH-SCRIPT

AIR

WARM
CULTURE
EXTROVERT
PASSIONATE
FUTURA

FIRE

EMOTIVE   TIN   IRON   EMOTIVE

N/EMOTIVE   COPPER   GOLD   N/EMOTIVE

BASKERVILLE
TRADITION
STABLE
EXECUTANT
WET

WATER

ROCKWELL
KNOW-HOW
REALIST
OBJECTIVE
DRY

EARTH

FEMININE   N/ACTIVE   ACTIVE   MASCULINE

Colour photocopiers and telecopiers have changed our lives, especially those of designers and communications specialists, but the graphic computer, which was introduced into DBB&P in 1983, is the most important element of the electronic revolution since the invention of printing. McLuhan goes even further by saying, 'This electronic revolution is only less confusing for men of the open societies than the revolution of phonetic literacy which stripped and streamlined the old tribal or closed societies'.[44]

In all areas the computer has completely revised the organization and the concept of work, not only by replacing man by a machine, but more importantly by increasing his potential and talent to an almost miraculous degree. Since the first computers, techniques and technology have evolved enormously and will continue to do so, which is why this chapter does not analyse current systems that will become quickly out-of-date. There are increasingly more seminars dealing with this, thus this chapter will simply try to define the principal functions of a computer in the packaging design business and the problems that arise.

7.1
THE MAIN FUNCTIONS OF THE GRAPHIC COMPUTER

The configuration of the main graphic computers is for the greater part the same; entry of outside elements by video camera, and the manipulation of the on-screen image using integrated functions employing a keypad and mouse or cursor, memorization of the results and output in the form of slides or hard copies. Whatever the type of problem, the process involves five essential functions common to all graphic computers: vocabulary, visualization, manipulation, memorization and output. The graphic computer may be thought of as a 'magic pencil' because it has a memory that can give instantaneous access to the potential normally found in a studio full of designers. It is 'magic' because it responds instantly to the wishes and demands of the designer, this immediacy being the chief characteristic of the electronic revolution.

7.1.1
A prodigious dictionary

Chapter 6 discussed the main elements of a package designer's vocabulary, and with minor differences the graphic computer has these same elements integrated into its memory, geometric shapes, textures, a huge colour spectrum, type, all combined with techniques that the designer uses in everyday life such as airbrush, enlargement and reduction, paste-up, cutting-out, distortion and superimposition etc.

Added to this rich basic vocabulary are elements specific to the job introduced by the video camera, this possibility of taking and using existing elements being a major advantage of the graphic computer, representing as it does the preparatory phase of a job.

7.1.2
Light images

The common factor of the visual arts is that of finding an idea and an appropriate way to present it, a creative process full of traps and disappointments very often resulting in the designer not being able to find a way to execute the idea as he had imagined it; or not bothering to develop it because he cannot see a viable solution; or he does not have the time or aptitude to do so. These situations waste time, effort and creativity, whereas a computer with its

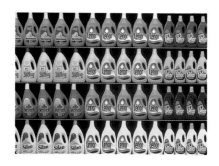

visualization speed can deliver an unhoped-for result by allowing the designer to look at all his ideas rapidly and often, while working, to inspire new ones, an element essential to creativity.

7.1.3
Dissecting the image

Manipulation and simulation are the graphic computer's two most spectacular functions, with the screen acting as a magic mirror that the designer uses to create and intermingle ideas to suit his creative wishes. It is possible both with shape and colour to cut the image, change the layout and analyse the different visual options possible. This technique is especially useful when trying to integrate a number of different elements. The designer can simulate multiples of a package and construct an on-shelf simulation to compare different solutions or to see how a design looks against competitive products.

7.1.4
The memory of an elephant

A computer cannot be a computer without its memory and in packaging design the facility of being able to recall an image or a creative stage from a previous job is ideal as it gives the designer access to his creative past, allowing him to look at previous ideas again or to modify or rework an existing concept in the light of a new problem. This continuous liaison with the visual memory constantly enriches creativity through the active interaction between man and machine.

7.1.5
Turning light into reality

Since the introduction of computers into package design these machines have become essentially a creative tool. However, even if the creative function is the leading one, it is obvious that the ideal machine would be capable of producing artwork as well, i.e. the material necessary to enable an engraver to produce film separations or gravure cylinders. Even if such a machine does not exist at present and one is currently obliged to use a creative computer and an artwork computer in parallel, there is no doubt, the two processes will eventually be combined, as the output of the two types of computer already surpasses anything that can be done by hand. A computer-generated transparency is of better quality than a project produced manually, and a plotter can draw artwork to an accuracy of 0.01 of a millimetre – somewhat better than a human being.

7.2
THE NEW DESIGNERS

'Nowadays a package designer can call up images on the screen almost instantaneously thanks to the speed of the machine, enabling him to try all kinds of possible solution and variation without the flow of creativity being broken by time constraints and technical limitations. Tomorrow's designer will be like a magician, exploring visual space with the speed of light, losing none of his talent, and increasing his creativity thanks to the infinite possibilities that electronics bring.' This was the conclusion to my speech to the 'The New Designer – Computer Graphics for Design' Seminar (New York, 1989). P. Jeffe, the organizer of this annual congress said in his introduction, 'The new tools have changed design technique forever – for the better – providing simplified visualization and presentation techniques, replacing the drawing board and eliminating the tedium of mechanicals.'

This congress, which brings together more than 400 designers, is living proof that the graphic computer has become part of our daily life, and designers have recognized the need to get together and discuss their experiences, problems and difficulties. Even if this new breed of designers can evolve in a way not possible in the past, there are special problems to be overcome, such as learning the 'logic' of how a computer works as well as becoming totally at ease with using the different functions; hopefully, something that art colleges will incorporate into their curricula. Finally, it is necessary to remain aware of the ways and the degree to which this revolution is changing our professional life and the way in which we work.

7.2.1
To each profession its computer

The type of work dictates the choice of computer, and in the 1980s it took me more than two years to find a computer that could be adapted to package design. Since then there has been an explosion in the market but even so there is a big difference in price and capability among the many machines available. In this fast-changing environment, it is useless to give a comparison chart, especially as magazines, for example *Computer Graphics* and *Computer Graphics World* adequately cover the subject. To evaluate a computer it must be tried out to see how well it performs the functions described above. Making a computer pay for itself means using it consistently, a question of identifying the type of work most suitable, such as repetitive adaptations, design of packaging ranges and complex corporate identity programmes.

7.2.2
Computers are expensive

Computers are not inexpensive and since investment in automation is something fairly new in the design business, it is worth calculating the implications both in medium and long term, taking into account the regular need either to update a system or to replace it by a more efficient one. A decent top-of-the-range computer currently costs in the region of US$150,000 and prices can vary enormously in function of the necessary peripherals. Experience shows that a computer used for more or less 80 per cent of available working time can pay for itself in two years.

7.2.3
Change the way you react

A computer completely changes the work pattern, the hourly price being at least twice that of a designer and varying in function of the type and volume of work. However, a computer enables much more to be achieved in less time, not necessarily the project taking less time, but enabling much more of that time to be applied to thinking as opposed to doing. The relationship between the designer and the machine is fundamental, as the designer must fully understand the binary logic of the machine in order to fully exploit its capabilities, using the best possible combinations of function to solve a given problem. With daily practice the designer can make the machine part of his thinking process, truly becoming a 'magic mirror', that most special of creative tools. Perhaps the most promising attribute of the computer is its potential to 'build bridges', that is to improve communication between designer and client, engraver and printer, which improves communication among everyone involved in the packaging development process.

7.2.4
Mastering the technique

A computer is a creative tool to be used by a designer and not by an operator, a solution that some manufacturers recommend, but which eliminates the essential spontaneous interaction between designer and machine. This obliges a design company to develop a continuous training programme capable of keeping designers up-to-date with the latest technology. The importance of this cannot be overestimated as the training support provided by computer companies is often inadequate, not to mention the lack of training provided by design schools (although this seems to be changing for the better).

7.2.5
The manufacturer/ designer relation- ship

The computer enables the manufacturer to have a better creative dialogue with the designer as certain of the presentation stages can be shown directly on computer, allowing the client to propose and evaluate additional solutions. The speed at which this can be done turns a passive presentation into an interactive work session, which is fine as long as the client does not believe that all the designer must do is press a button and a design appears instantly.

One cannot emphasize enough the importance of the preparatory work necessary before beginning a computer design job, not just entering visual elements into the memory, but the large amount of thought and analysis that is required (Chapter 5). The ratio is 20:80 with 80 per cent thought for 20 per cent design work.

The production stage is the ultimate phase of a package design project, and depending on the care and quality that has been applied, is either the 'crowning' moment or a failure. Many years ago a department was created within DBB&P whose sole responsibility is to ensure that creative jobs are carried out properly, meticulously and with outstanding creativity throughout. In order to ensure that a job proceeds correctly it should begin with a pre-production meeting between the client, the production department and the creative group, in order to determine the technical criteria and limitations so that they can be adhered to throughout the project to the artwork stage and finally the checking of the printed proofs.

8.1

SEPARATE THE POSSIBLE FROM THE IMPOSSIBLE

The pre-production meeting is for all those involved in the project and enables them to discuss the different technical aspects of the assignment; also it is equally valuable for the designer, technician and printer to clearly understand the objectives and above all the technical limitations, and 'impossibilities'. Sometimes technicians can destroy a good idea, saying that it is impossible while refusing to look at the problem in a different light. However, machines do have their limitations and the designer and production people should be aware of them, as sometimes a creative mind can use these limitations to find a new solution to a problem.

Printing half-tone backgrounds in four-colour separation, especially when the colour must be accurate to identify a specific variety, can present problems, but these can be solved by using only two or three colours, something an engraver or printer will not necessarily think of. Bottle manufacture, either in plastic or glass, involves the use of very complex moulds and very high production speeds. In the space available it is impossible to review all potential problems inherent in the numerous manufacturing and printing processes, and it is this very complexity that is the reason for having a production meeting.

8.2

THE IDEA MADE CONCRETE

The role of the production department is to finalize (i.e. to 'crown') a package design project. This is the most critical and difficult phase, where an omission or error can ruin the overall quality, hence nothing less than excellence is acceptable.

Even if an attempt is made to understand the complexity of packaging, the designer's visual language; the importance of his knowledge and his varied talents will lead to nothing if the artwork is imprecise, or badly thought out or simply badly executed. The indispensable elements are the technical drawing, the final text and any necessary translations, the brand graphics, usage, legal text, illustrations – all the graphic or typographic elements that constitute the package. Often at this stage

things go wrong, either because of lack of time, organization or coordination, and although changes can be made, they often involve many extra hours of work or even preparation of new artwork.

As in the creative area, the graphic computer is replacing traditional artwork methods and the same considerations apply to an artwork computer as to one that is used in graphics. In addition to the approximate six-month period necessary to train an operator, the

workflow organization is very important, needing a large throughput that is as repetitive as possible, since the construction of basic elements is fairly slow and generally more costly than preparing them by hand, and it is when using and adapting elements that are in the memory that the computer shows its own capabilities.

The other side of the final artwork is the choice and co-ordination of the elements that constitute the design, such as type, illustration

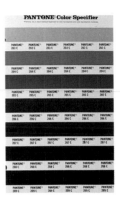

and photography; thus, it is essential to work with specialists in order to achieve the best possible result.

When finished, the artwork should be supplied complete with a colour guide, providing the engraver with the necessary information to enable preparation of the colour separation films in order to make plates or gravure cylinders. Nowadays it is possible to supply artwork directly from the computer on magnetic tape, although obviously only if the artwork meets with the client's approval.

8.3
TASTE AND COLOUR

Colour and its importance to packaging were discussed in section 6.1.3. The role of the colour guide is important in that it is responsible for ensuring that the printer produces the result required by the designer. The PANTONE®* MATCHING SYSTEM is recommended as an aid. This has nine basic colours which can be mixed to produce 747 different colours, each identified by a number corresponding to its chromatic composition. Of the 747 colours, 500 can be matched using four-colour separation, and even if 747 colours do not seem many compared to the thousands that a designer can mix or generate on a graphic computer, they are in fact

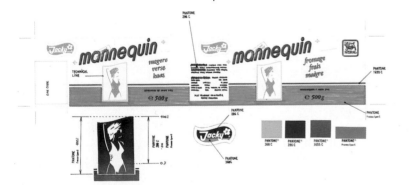

* Pantone, Inc.'s check-standard trademark for color reproduction and color reproduction materials.

sufficient and are internationally recognized. Sometimes there may be difficulties in matching colours, either produced by traditional means or when generated in red, green and blue (RGB) on a computer as they must be translated into an equivalent produced from magenta, cyan, yellow and black; the surface they are printed on and the lighting also play a role. 'The reproduction of a colour can only be perfect if the material on which it is printed is identical to the original... The same image looks very different depending on whether it is printed on a matt or glossy surface.'[45] All this emphasizes the importance of correct specification and control.

8.4
EASY READING

A large part of the population suffers from impaired vision and for this reason it is important not to use text that is either too small or printed on a background colour that renders it illegible, such as white on yellow or green on orange; out of respect for the consumer, text should be readable. Often the amount of text makes this difficult, but by combining a readable typeface with an easy-to-read colour it is possible to achieve acceptable legibility. Text should be replaced by a symbol whenever possible.

8.5
PRESENT AT THE BIRTH

For a project to be a success, the production manager and creative director should check pre-production package samples or printed proofs and time should be allotted in the project schedule in order to allow corrections or refinements to be made; sometimes another production meeting may be required. At the start of a print run the production manager generally goes to the printer with the client to ensure that any corrections or refinements are incorporated. The artwork and colour guide are used as the basis to check the printed result, and where questions of brand identity arise, they should be checked against the brand identity manual.

8.6
TECHNOLOGY ON THE MOVE

Without considering developing technologies such as ionic bombardment, magnetographics and electronic photography,[46] the traditional printing methods of offset, gravure, flexography and screen are constantly evolving both in quality and range of application. The entire graphics business, photocomposition, photogravure, retouching and

printing, has been revolutionized not only by electronics, but also by the wide range and variety of glues, inks and varnishes available. Several areas where creative use of technology has affected packaging are as follows:

1 Electronic thermal transfer which gives extra depth to labels or packages in card or plastic by adding a gold or silver layer.

2 Heat-shrunk printed film sleeves used on glass, plastic or metal packages, replacing printing on the package itself, giving a larger surface area for graphics, and sometimes even used as a form of additional protection or insulation.

3 The traditional metal can which is now produced with forms other than the straight cylindrical one especially for beers and foods and sometimes with the body made of laminated board or plastic rather than metal, the ends being pressed out of aluminium sheet.

4 Portion or dose-size products have required innovative packaging as with microwave meals where the meal is cooked in its package.

Modern packaging would not be what it is without the invention of corrugated carton, blow moulding, twist-off caps, cluster paks, aerosols and Tetra Brik packs as well as numerous other systems. However, there are many innovative developments to come.

It could be said that the brand is more important to the product than the company that manufactures it, and that packaging is the best support that the brand can have, since its function is to disseminate the product throughout the world – a package is essentially 'international'. Because of the ever-growing international nature of the media and other areas of human activity, it has become increasingly important to address packaging to as wide an audience as possible. To speak of regional packaging is an anachronism even though a product may have a regional association, as is the case with French champagne, Swiss cheese, Portuguese port or German beer. It is almost certain that any product could be sold anywhere in the world using the same packaging as long as the national language, legislation and habits are taken into consideration. Most products that we buy today are international whether they be cars, clothes, cigarettes, beers, detergents, perfumes, wine, coffee, chocolates, etc; it is a fact that multinationals and most national companies (especially in Europe) understand the importance of the European and global market. However, out of all the brands on the market, there are few that will truly succeed in becoming global, and even if a brand is visually well-thought-out and organized, it must be manufactured by a

company with an internal structure capable of appreciating and managing this extraordinary asset.

9.1

A REAL BRAND IS INTERNATIONAL

The objective of a co-ordination structure is to be able to launch the same product using the same packaging simultaneously in a number of different countries, taking into account local marketing needs and setting up as short a decision-making chain as possible. In these circumstances the package design brief should be handled by a co-ordinator who then seeks the comments of the different local managers, but keeps to one brief which then acts as a common denominator even to the way in which the brand personality is translated. This can only be achieved when a company applies a common, consistent brand policy, and has the will to enforce it and to make it respected, thus preventing people from 'tampering' with the brand image. To do this, a company needs a 'world' brand co-ordinator backed, if necessary, by 'regional' co-ordinators responsible for communication with headquarters (Europe, USA, Latin America, Africa, etc.).

This approach should not exclude regional variations, such as the use of different recipe illustrations for soups or pre-prepared meals, as long as there is a strong graphic structure which reinforces the visual relationship between different products with the same brand name.

The diagrams below illustrate the crucial moments in the co-ordination process: the first is the preparation of a common brief and the second the decision-making phase, with each one being simultaneous. As was noted in Chapter 5, qualitative testing is generally used between the creative phase and the final execution as a decision-making aid.

DECISION PROCESS

INFORMATION	DESIGN	TEST	FINAL ART	PRODUCTION
BRIEFING	DESIGN PRESENTATION TO LEAD COUNTRY	QUALITATIVE TESTS	PRE-PRODUCTION MEETING	PRODUCTION MEETING (ENGRAVER-PRINTER)
	COMMUNICATE DESIGN PROPOSAL TO ALL COUNTRIES		PREPARATION OF FINAL ART	FIRST PROOF APPROVAL
TECHNICAL INPUT	DESIGN APPROVAL		FINAL ART APPROVALS (ART - TECHNICAL - LEGAL)	PRINTING

WORKFLOW

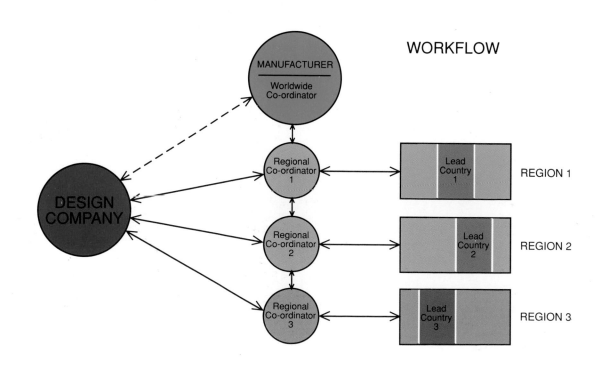

9.2
A COHERENT IDEA

Where a brand management structure exists, it brings two benefits: the first ensures proper control of the brand on an international level, the second the large-scale economies it generates.

9.2.1
The brand equity

Not only does the co-ordinator assemble marketing information and prepare the design brief, but he must also ensure that the brand image is applied as set down in the brand identity manual. This somewhat difficult role of 'guard dog' is vital if the brand image is to be used in a consistent way in different countries, whatever the medium used.

9.2.2
Co-ordination is money

Co-ordinating a brand on an international level using one design studio represents an enormous saving in energy and effort by avoiding duplication of design work, of meetings, of re-inventing the wheel and by simplifying the decision-making process (see above). The most impressive economies are those of scale due to the increased quantities that result from centralized production, which reduces the unit cost while making communication between client and supplier much simpler by limiting the number of engravers and printers they must deal with. As packaging is often in four-colour separation and often multilingual, centralization allows a rationalization of the number of sizes and versions needed to cover the different markets. Given that a gravure cylinder costs around US$2000, the savings both in money and manpower can be considerable, especially taking into account the fact that manpower and energy are becoming more scarce.

In spite of the fact that worldwide brand co-ordination is a relatively new marketing dimension for many companies, it has become a fundamental part of controlling the large brands of the future, and is now an important factor in package design.

Packaging communication is the domain of signs and symbols, as their conciseness eliminates the need for long or complex explanations.

A package can be destroyed by promotions; the anarchic use of graphic elements ruins visual unity and brand image.

A package is neither a poster nor an advertisement. An excellent advertisement can make a worthless package. Both communicate the same promise but in different ways.

A package cannot be evaluated on a conference room table; only in its natural sales environment.

A package is not designed to last forever, and must evolve continuously to keep pace with the market and consumer tastes.

A complex pack is not noticed.

A well-designed pack costs much less than a badly-thought-out, or non-thought-out package. Any well-designed package is the result of a good brief.

A brand can pass from year to year as long as the product continues to perform and to satisfy the consumer. The package, as a commercial object, has a role to play in the evolution of contemporary aesthetics, and is a cultural object as well as a 'commercial work of art'.

The package is the 'face' of a product, and a product without a brand name lacks substance because of its lack of personality.

Colour can make a package lighter, richer, warmer, colder, more masculine or feminine, more calm or more natural, etc.

Colour used in packaging has no individual value. Its essential role is to give individuality to the product and make it stand out from the competition.

An image, even an attractive one, is not sufficient to make a package a good one.

Execution is a fundamental phase of creative packaging.

A package knows no frontiers, and is international by nature.

A package in a mass display is different from a package placed on its own.

The package is the least expensive form of advertising per client contact.

A package protects, transports, presents, attracts, informs, explains, sells, satisfies, etc., but above all communicates the brand identity.

A good package will not sell a bad product for long.

A package may follow fashion … but fashion is constantly changing.

In conclusion, it is hoped that this book helps to further a better understanding of brand packaging, and above all makes decision-makers aware of what an important business tool a package is.

'More than ever the symbol will replace the word, visual images, mainly through packaging, will become the international passport for recognition and understanding. In our tumultuous world the corporate identity will be and will remain the key asset of corporate "reality". Increasing competition will make it more and more difficult to be seen in the crowd, to be identified as the specialist in one's field, or simply to be considered as a possible purchase. We are slowly but surely entering into a total communication process. Media will allow us to travel everywhere and faster than any transportation system. The world is shrinking. Any company and any product should be instantly on the market anywhere, providing they are recognizable, which means that the identity must be understood the same way everywhere.

How many brands or companies are really consistent with their image? Very few of them and this is why the real challenge of tomorrow will not be to be everywhere at once, but to be *recognized* everywhere through the same signature.'[47]

It is then and only then that as a permanent medium the package can play its role as a 'persuasive salesman', a real ambassador for the manufacturer, because the package and the brand identity are the same thing.

REFERENCES

1 'The World of Packaging', booklet published by J. Behaeghel, 1977, Chapter 1.

2 *Colour Sells Your Package*, Pilditch, (J.-P. Favre), Editions ABC, Zürich, 1969, p.131.

3 *The Medium is the Message*, M. McLuhan and Q. Fiore, Penguin Books, Harmondsworth, 1967, p.63.

4 *Le Saut Créatif*, J.-M. Dru, Editions Jean-Claude Lattès, France, 1984, p.21.

5 *La Marque*, J.N. Kapferer and J.C. Thoenig, McGraw-Hill, Paris, 1989, p.22.

6 *Le Saut Créatif*, J.-M. Dru, Editions Jean-Claude Lattès, France, 1984, p.233.

7 *Colour Sells Your Package*, J.-P. Favre, Editions ABC, Zürich, 1969, p.35.

8 Brand, Innovation and Economic Growth, B. Yon, in *La Marque* (J.N. Kapferer and J.C. Thoenig), McGraw-Hill, Paris, 1989, p.267.

9 *Le Pack*, CEP Communication, BSN Emballage, Paris, 1987, p.19.

10 *Manifeste*, J. de Noblet, Asnières, 1989, p.36.

11 Packaging and Environment, *World Packaging News*, P. Schmit, July 1989, p.2.

12 *La Persuasion Clandestine*, V. Packard, Calmann-Lévy, Mayenne, 1989, p.11.

13 New Generation of Consumers, *World Packaging News*, September 1989, p.1.

14 *Le Saut Créatif*, J.-M. Dru, Editions Jean-Claude Lattès, France, 1984, p.38.

15 Introduction, F. Dalle in *La Marque* (J.N. Kapferer and J.C. Thoenig), McGraw-Hill, Paris, 1989, p.xviii.

16 Sensibility to Brands, J.N. Kapferer and G. Laurent in *La Marque* (J.N. Kapferer and J.C. Thoenig), McGraw-Hill, Paris, 1989, pp.112–113.

17 *Le Saut Créatif*, J.-M. Dru, Editions Jean-Claude Lattès, France, 1984, p.32.

18 Brand Product and Communication, J.N. Kapferer in *La Marque* (J.N. Kapferer and J. C. Thoenig), McGraw-Hill, Paris, 1989, p.29.

19 *Colour Sells Your Package*, J.-P. Favre, Editions ABC, Zürich, 1969, p.31.

20 *La Persuasion Clandestine*, V. Packard, Calmann-Lévy, Mayenne, 1989, p.49.

21 Concepts and Brand Strategies in Japan, M. Yoshimori in *La Marque* (J.N. Kapferer and J.C. Thoenig), McGraw-Hill, Paris, 1989, p.291.

22 *Le Marketing Guerrier*, A. Ries and J. Trout, McGraw-Hill, Paris, 1988, p.129.

23 Beauté et Laideur, G. Patrix in *Nouvelle Encyclopédie*, Hachette, Paris, 1967, pp.6 and 29.

24 *Colour Sells Your Package*, J.-P. Favre, Editions ABC, Zürich, 1969, p.19.

25 The Packaging Components, CEP Communication, in *Le Pack*, BSN Emballage, Paris, 1987, p.45.

26 *Packaging (Design in Motion)*, Stewart Mosberg, PBC Inter-national Inc., New York, 1989.

27 Beauté et Laideur, G. Patrix in *Nouvelle Encyclopédie*, Hachette, Paris, 1967, p.92.

28 *Le Langage des Couleurs*, R.L. Rousseau, Editions Dangles, France.

29 *Colour*, P. Zelanski and M. P. Fisher, The Herbert Press, London, 1989, p.128.

30 *Colour Sells Your Package*, J.-P. Favre, Editions ABC, Zürich, 1969, pp.72 and 73.

31 *Dictionnaire des Symboles*, J. Chevalier and A. Gheerbrant, Robert Laffont/Jupiter, Paris, 1969 and 1982, p.294.

32 *Le Signe*, U. Eco, Collection Média, Editions Labor, Bruxelles, 1988, p.59.

33 *The Gütenberg Galaxy*, M. McLuhan, Routledge & Kegan Paul, London, 1962, pp.164 and 241.

34 *Type and Colour*, M. Beaumont, Phaidon Press, London, 1987, p.12.

35 *Type and Colour*, M. Beaumont, Phaidon Press, London, 1987, p.28.

36 *Heraldic Design*, H. Child, G. Bell and Sons, London, 1970.

37 *La Persuasion Clandestine*, V. Packard, Calmann-Lévy, Mayenne, 1989, p.81.

38 *Theory and Use of Colour*, L. de Grandis, Blandford Press, Bole-Dorset, 1986, p.27.

39 *La Caractérologie*, G. Palmade, Presses Universitaires de France, Paris, 1981, pp.103–108.

40 *Colour Sells Your Package*, J.-P. Favre, Editions ABC, Zürich, 1969, pp.19 and 21.

41 *Le Signe*, U. Eco, Collection Média, Editions Labor, Bruxelles, 1988, p.137.

42 *Le Saut Créatif*, J.-M. Dru, Editions Jean-Claude Lattès, France, 1984, p.150.

43 *Colour*, P. Zelanski and M. P. Fisher, The Herbert Press, London, 1989, p.33.

44 *The Gütenberg Galaxy*, M. McLuhan, Routledge & Kegan Paul, London, 1962, p.8.

45 *Les Applications Nouvelles des Procédés d'Impression*, P. Durchon, Editions du Moniteur, Paris, 1989, p.41.

46 *Les Applications Nouvelles des Procédés d'Impression*, P. Durchon, Editions du Moniteur, Paris, 1989, p.171.

47 When Image Becomes Reality, *Business Strategy International*, J. Behaeghel, Cornhill Publications, Winter 1989–90, p.37.

LIST OF ILLUSTRATIONS

After Eight	Danette	Kenzo
Amora	Danino	Kirin
Ariel	Dany	Kleenex
Baby Gal	Dash 3	Knorr
Baby Soft	D'Aucy	Kodak
Balvenie	Delhaize	Koipe
Bass	Del Monte	Kraft
Bayer	Design Board/Behaeghel & Partners	Kronenbourg
Beaumont	(DBB&P)	Lacoste
Beefeater	Dextro Energy	L'Alsacienne
Bière des Druides	Dr Oetker	Laurent Perrier
Binon J.	Douwe Egberts	Leo
Bleu Rio	Ducados	Lenor
BN/Choc Coeur	Dunhill	Liebig
Boursault	Effi	Lipton
Bridel	Epi d'Or	Lite
Brise	Evian	Loburg
Brochet	Fabergé	Los Hermanos
Brut	Findus	Looza
Café in bottle	Galettes de Lanester (Albert Menes)	Lotus
Camel	Gauloises	Lu
Canderel	Gillette	Lucky Strike
Carlsberg	Gitanes	Luvs
Carte Brasserie (William Saurin)	Godiva	Mahou
Cartier	Granini	Maison du Café
Cassegrain	Gucci	Maizena
Ça-va-seul	Guerlain	Maja (Myrurgia)
Cepsa	Heineken	Mannequin
Cerelac	Heinz	Mariana Light
Chambourcy	Henkell Trocken	Marie Brizard
Chaudfontaine	Hero	Marlboro
Chivas Regal	IBM	Meister Brau
Choc (Cardin)	Iglo	Metaltex
Ciments d'Obourg	Interbrew	Miau (Alfageme)
Cluster Pak	Jacksons of Piccadilly	Miaou
Coca-Cola	Jacky	Miko
Coral	Jacqmotte	Milka
Côte d'Or	Johnnie Walker	Miller Lite
CPC	Johnson Wax	Minute Maid
Cubitainer	Kango	Mon Chéri
Danone	Kellogg's	Monsanto

Monsavon

Mr Muscle

Mr Propre

Nabisco/Belin

Nadler

Nescafé

Nesquik

Nestlé

Nielsen

Nivea

Nutricia

Nutrimel

Nutri-Soja

Ny Rost (Gevalia)

Obernai

Oë

Oil of Olaz (Oil of Ulay)

Omo

Orangina

Ovomaltine

Paluani

Pampers

PANTONE®*

Patek Philippe

Pepito

Pepsi Cola

Perrier

Persil

Perwoll

Petit Navire

Petit Pansey

Petit Plat Gourmand (Barbier Dauphin)

Primus

Prince Noir (Nestlé)

Procter & Gamble

Pouss' Mousse

Quaker Oats

Radion

Remy Martin

Riblaire (Chèvre Cœur)

Rush

Saimaza

Sandeman

Sapporo

Saupiquet

Schweppes

Season

Shell (Puissance 5)

Snack Bar

Spa

Squires

Stella Artois

Stroh's

Sucreries de Tirlemont

Sun

Sunland

Sunlight

Suntory

Sylphide

Tahiti

Terruzi & Puthod

Tetra Brik

Tide

Ti'Light

Tonigencyl

Twist-Off

Uncle Ben's

Unilever

Vache qui rit

Valensina

Vandemoortele

Vittel

Vizir

W.C. Canard

Wilson's

Xeryus

Yves St Laurent

Yarden

Young & Rubicam

*Pantone, Inc.'s check-standard trademark
for color reproduction and color reproduction
materials.